Dance Talking Dance

Critical Evaluation in the Choreography Class

Larry Lavender, PhD
University of New Mexico, Albuquerque

Human Kinetics

Library of Congress Cataloging-in-Publication Data

Lavender, Larry, 1954-
    Dancers talking dance : critical evaluation in the choreography
class / Larry Lavender.
        p.   cm.
    Includes bibliographical references and index.
    ISBN 0-87322-667-4   ,
    1. Dance criticism.   2. Choreography--Study and teaching.
I. Title.
GV1600.L38   1996
792.82--dc20   95-49233
                                                           CIP

ISBN: 0-87322-667-4

Brief passages of this book have been modified, with permission of the publishers, from material that first appeared in the author's articles "Learning to 'See' Dance: The Role of Critical Writing in Developing Students' Aesthetic Awareness," which appeared in *Impulse*, vol. 1, no. 1, July, 1993, pp. 10-20, and "Critical Evaluation in the Choreography Class," which appeared in *Dance Research Journal*, vol. 24, no. 2, Fall, 1992.

Acquisitions and Developmental Editor: Judy Patterson Wright, PhD; **Assistant Editor:** John Wentworth; **Editorial Assistant:** Jennifer Hemphill; **Copyeditor:** Jacqueline Eaton Blakley; **Proofreader:** Jacqueline L. Seebaum; **Indexer:** Mary Lavender; **Typesetting and Layout:** Ruby Zimmerman; **Text Designer:** Robert Reuther; **Cover Designer:** Jack Davis; **Photographer (cover):** © Jack Vartoogian; **Photographer (interior):** Keith Drosin; **Photo Models:** Jillian Bird, Larry Lavender, Kaeti Miller, Maki Nishiyama, Jessica Vandebroek; **Printer:** Versa Press

Printed in the United States of America   10 9 8 7 6 5 4 3 2 1

Human Kinetics
P.O. Box 5076, Champaign, IL 61825-5076
1-800-747-4457

Canada: Human Kinetics, Box 24040, Windsor, ON N8Y 4Y9
1-800-465-7301 (in Canada only)

Europe: Human Kinetics, P.O. Box IW14, Leeds LS16 6TR, United Kingdom
(44) 1132 781708

Australia: Human Kinetics, 2 Ingrid Street, Clapham 5062, South Australia
(08) 371 3755

New Zealand: Human Kinetics, P.O. Box 105-231, Auckland 1
(09) 523 3462

CONTENTS

Foreword   vi

Preface   viii

Acknowledgments   x

Introduction   1
    The ORDER Approach to Critical Evaluation   2
    Critical Evaluation Is a Language Art   3
    The ORDER Approach Facilitates Critical Thinking Skills   4
    How This Book Is Organized   6

**Part I Perspectives on Critical Evaluation
in Dance Education**   **8**

Chapter 1 Criticism Within the Choreography Class   **11**
    Casual Conversation and Critical Discourse   13
    Choreography Is a Revisions Process   16
    The Choreography Classroom as an Art World   20
    Summary: Important Points to Remember   21

Chapter 2 The Subjective Response   **23**
    Subjectivity and the Viewer's Role as Audience Member   24
    The Nature of the Subjectivist Approach   25
    Confusion About Feelings in Art   27
    The Pitfalls of Subjectivist Reasoning   27
    Overcoming Subjectivism: The Essential Question to Ask   28
    The Role of Subjectivity in the Critical Process   29
    Summary: Important Points to Remember   30

Chapter 3 The Problem of Using Predetermined Criteria   **31**
    The Risks of Predetermined Criteria   32
    The Risks of Theory-Based Criteria   35
    Compounding the Risks: Predetermined Discussion
        Questions   35
    Summary: Important Points to Remember   37

Chapter 4   The Problem of Relying on Artists' Intentions   **39**
   The Concept of Intention   40
   Communication and Dance   42
   The Use of Intentions in Critical Evaluation   44
   Summary: Important Points to Remember   47

Chapter 5   Teacher Myths About Critical Evaluation   **49**
   Myth #1: "It's the Teacher's Job to Tell Students What's Good."   50
   Myth #2: "Hearing Criticism Hurts Students' Feelings."   52
   Myth #3: "Dancers Should Do Dancing, Not Discuss It."   53
   Myth #4: "Students Learn to Critique Dances
     by Making Dances."   55
   Summary: Important Points to Remember   57

Part II The ORDER Approach to Critical Evaluation   58

Chapter 6   Observation   **61**
   Perceptual Openness   62
   Noticing Versus Recognizing   63
   Sample Observation Exercise   64
   Summary: Important Points to Remember   65

Chapter 7   Reflection   **67**
   The Goals of Reflective Writing   69
   Initiating Focused Freewriting   69
   Describing the Dance   70
   The Danger of Critical Assumptions   72
   Analyzing Relationships   73
   The Importance of Reflection   75
   The Choreographer's Role During Reflection   76
   Summary: Important Points to Remember   77

Chapter 8   Discussion   **79**
   The Importance of Sharing Reflective Notes   81
   Discussion Stage 1: Description and Analysis   81
   Discussion Stage 2: Interpretation   82
   Artists' Contributions to Interpretive Discussion   84
   General Explanations and Artistic Justifications   85
   Summary: Important Points to Remember   87

Chapter 9   Evaluation   **89**
  The Concept of Judgment   90
  Evaluative Pluralism   92
  The Ladder of Aesthetic Inquiry   94
  Summary: Important Points to Remember   99

Chapter 10   Recommendations for Revisions   **101**
  Critical Projection   102
  Recommending Revisions Versus "Fixing" the Dance   103
  Post-Revision Review   104
  The Importance of Deferring Revision Recommendations   105
  Summary: Important Points to Remember   107

Part III   Implementation of the ORDER Approach   108

Chapter 11   Skill Level Distinctions in Choreography Courses   111
  Typical Choreography Assignments for Beginners   112
  Presented and Discovered Problems   113
  Critical Projection With Beginners   115
  Typical Choreography Assignments for Advanced Students   116
  Discovered-Problem Situations   118
  Summary: Important Points to Remember   119

Chapter 12   Potential Obstacles to Critical Evaluation   121
  Handling Anticritical Beliefs and Attitudes   122
  Handling Critical Disagreements   125
  Linguistic and Rhetorical Causes of Disagreement   127
  The Remedy for Linguistic and Rhetorical Disagreements   130
  Summary: Important Points to Remember   130

Afterword   **132**
Bibliography   **134**
Index   **146**
About the Author   **148**

FOREWORD

It is another day in choreography class, and the teacher and students are watching the latest group of studies created by the students. The first student volunteers, shows her work, and anxiously awaits feedback. Following a familiar period of awkward silence, the teacher prods the students who have just watched the study.

"Well, what do you think?"

Reluctantly, someone offers, "It was good. I liked it," and then falls silent.

And so it begins again—the teacher's and students' quest for meaningful discussion about the dance work, the process that resulted in its creation, and whether appropriate artistic choices have been made by the dancer. This classroom scenario is common to all of us who teach choreography courses, ranging from improvisation to providing artistic mentoring to students producing their own work.

Larry's book brings to the field of dance education a method of critiquing in the choreography class that far surpasses the familiar checklists and craft-oriented questions, which may or may not have relevance to the work being considered. At the core of this book is the understanding that dance works are potentially full of meanings, rather than meaning one thing in particular. When we watch dance, we have many possibilities of interpretation, and the journey toward understanding a dance work is a process of entering the world created by the choreographer. The process presented in this book recognizes that all works are crafted, though they may be crafted in far different ways; that while movement may be the common denominator, movement as a medium of expression means different things to different people; and that the work creates its own frame for viewing and valuing the dance. Critical discourse in the choreography class involves discovering the world created by the choreographer, entering that world, and trying to evaluate how well that world was created and what might make it more engaging, meaningful, or compelling.

The process Larry has developed encourages students by giving credibility to *their* perceptions and interpretations and by placing the teacher and student in a relationship characterized by mutuality, respect for diverse points of view, and a common desire to make justified judgments. In such a situation, teachers must give up some of their authority and be prepared to negotiate terrain outside clearly defined markers. However, if the focus remains on the work, as Larry's method encourages, then the process of observation-reflection-discussion-evaluation-revision allows all who watch the dance to shape their own journeys toward understanding it. Just as we value the development of individual creative voice in dance making, we should foster the development of this attribute regarding how our students perceive, interpret, and discuss dance works.

The paradox of teaching choreography is that our students must enter in without knowing in order to discover what they need to know about the work they are creating. When dancers talk about dance in the context of dance making, the circle is complete—making, perceiving, reflecting, interpreting, evaluating, and then remaking *with greater understanding*.

Penelope Hanstein, PhD
Texas Woman's University
Denton, Texas

PREFACE

As a dancer and choreographer, I am always interested in hearing feedback from people who see my work. Unfortunately, most people— including college and university dance students—are uncomfortable talking to artists about their work because they have had no formal training in either analyzing or discussing works of art. Unsure of what to say, people usually give little or no response to the work, leaving the artist disappointed by the apparent lack of reaction.

A number of years ago I decided to find a solution to this problem. While teaching choreography in a university dance department, I began asking teachers of music, theater, and art how they structured critical talk in their classes. I also set aside one hour each week to teach my students how to talk critically about the dances they were making and observing in our class. And I began reading works on criticism in order to formulate a systematic approach to structuring dance talk in the choreography class.

In many classes since that time, I have continued to refine my approach to teaching students to deliver clear, precise, and useful critical feedback to their peers. It soon became clear that certain aspects of the critical process need detailed explanation, while others do not. I began to see, through working with students, what needs to happen first to facilitate critical discussion, what should happen next, and what should be saved for last. Above all, I discovered that students are able to learn how to discuss dances and, moreover, that they enjoy and profit from doing so once they know how.

This book and the approach it outlines are the result of my years of thinking and learning about critical evaluation in the choreography class. Teachers and students of choreography who read and discuss this approach to critical evaluation will discover that talking meaningfully about dances (and other works of art) is not as hard as it seems. They will become more perceptive observers, more reflective thinkers, more effective writers, and more articulate speakers about their art.

In this book, critical evaluation—that is, systematic and focused talk about each dance seen in class—is conceived of as a pedagogical *method* to be employed in the choreography course, not as a pedagogical *goal* of the course. This distinction is important, for there are educational aims to be achieved in any choreography course beyond simply becoming proficient at critical evaluation. Indeed, the choreography course is a creative learning laboratory for dance, not a course on dance criticism. Thus, my approach includes a series of critical actions to be performed by students in order to achieve the wider educational aims of helping choreographers understand and improve their works-in-progress. The improved critical feedback that student choreographers give to and receive from each other by using this approach helps them not only to make better dances, but to make them with greater confidence. These latter two aims are the fundamental goals of the choreography class.

A method for critical evaluation in choreography and dance education is needed now more than ever. New National Arts Standards require students at all levels to develop critical thinking skills in tandem with creative art-making skills. New tensions in society about the role, value, and meaning of art demand that college-trained artists be able not only to speak and write clearly about the importance of their work, but to teach the next generation of students how to do these things as well. By teaching choreography students how to analyze and evaluate dances and how to articulate these analyses and evaluations, the approach outlined in this book helps to prepare dance students for the future. It develops in students the skills that will be necessary if they are to join in, and contribute to, the ongoing discourse among dance educators, historians, critics, and practicing artists who continually explore and illuminate the vitality of dance.

To my wife, Elisabeth, and our little angel, Bridget Elaine

Acknowledgments

I owe an enormous debt of gratitude to Debra L. Zaller, whose perceptive questions and sound advice kept me on track as I developed this manuscript. I also extend sincere appreciation to my students at the University of Missouri-Kansas City, New York University, and the University of New Mexico who have participated in my testing of the new critical approach. I hope they realize how deeply their insights have influenced my own. Finally, I wish to thank my developmental editor at Human Kinetics, Dr. Judy Patterson Wright, for her endless patience and thoughtful guidance.

INTRODUCTION

In the typical choreography class, a teacher leads improvisations and makes assignments and the students produce small dances, or choreographic "studies." The students present their dances to the class so they can hear feedback that will help them improve their creative efforts. In addition, showing their dances to the class helps students develop their capacity to observe and evaluate dances.

There are thus two distinct but interdependent practices in which choreography students are expected to gain proficiency during the course. The first is producing compositional studies, which involves exploring and making creative choices about movement, structure, and meaning in the dance. The second is *critical evaluation*, which involves verbally describing, analyzing, interpreting, and judging works made by others in the class.

Instruction in critical evaluation is, unfortunately, often neglected in the choreography class. The professional literature available to choreography teachers focuses primarily on improvisations and movement-design exercises and often provides lists of qualities considered essential to "good" dances. But until now, very little professional guidance on critical evaluation has been available to teachers. This book provides such guidance. Moreover, it overturns the traditional view of the choreography student as one who engages in, and whose own work is subject to, substantive critical evaluation only occasionally and in a very restricted manner. Instead, student choreographers are viewed as interactive participants in the creation, evaluation, and revision of their own and others' choreographic products.

The ORDER Approach to Critical Evaluation

My approach to critical evaluation in the choreography class is called the ORDER approach. It begins with an *Observation* phase. During observation, one carefully and consciously sees, or attends to, the work of art. Next is a period of *Reflective* writing during which viewers describe and analyze the aesthetic object or experience. Only after reflection does a *Discussion* phase take place. The discussion stage of critical evaluation has two parts: First, students share reflective notes; then they formulate and discuss interpretations of the meaning and significance of the dance.

Discussion continues in the fourth stage of critical evaluation, the *Evaluation* stage. Here judgments of the work are articulated and debated. Evaluation is a distinct step in the critical process because it is important to defer judgment until the latter stages of a critique.

Because the choreographic process relies so heavily on revising and reassessing works-in-progress, the fifth step of the critical process is a two-part process for *Revision* of the work. First, viewers recommend how the work might be reshaped; then they assess the revised dance.

As all choreography teachers can attest, viewers untrained in critical evaluation tend to formulate interpretations and judgments immediately following, or even during, their initial observation of a work of art. Yet when viewers are asked to provide specific support for their initial reactions, they usually recall only general perceptions about the work. And what they recall usually happens to buttress the conclusions they have already reached. Features of the work that might contradict those viewers' verdicts are generally forgotten, downplayed, or ignored. This is why, in the ORDER approach, descriptions and analyses must be consciously formulated through reflective writing *before* interpretations and judgments are rendered. Descriptions and analyses considered during the first part of the discussion stage form the basis of understanding from which interpretations and judgments can be formulated, justified, and delivered to others.

There are two criteria necessary for valid interpretations and aesthetic judgments:

1. The viewer's interpretations and judgments cannot be contradicted by any visible features of the work.
2. No judgments or interpretations may be stated for which there is no visible basis *in the work*.

Critical Evaluation Is a Language Art

Drawing on approaches to critical evaluation already in place in aesthetics and in the philosophy of art, the ORDER approach to critical evaluation is based on the idea that to respond critically to a dance, or any work of art, is to discuss it—to put into words one's experience of the work. Only through the clear articulation of one's critical views can one accomplish the fundamental aims of critical evaluation: to improve others' ability both to see and to appreciate the work under review. This means that to be a good critic one must both verbally identify the visible properties of the work and make persuasive arguments for the meanings and merits one finds in the work.

Obviously, the critical process is not simply one of delivering instant opinions about a work of art. Instead, the viewer must first focus on the work in a concentrated manner and, later, engage in reflective consideration of the work's aesthetic properties. Only then is one truly in a position to engage in substantive critical discourse about the work.

By teaching dance viewers how to observe, describe, analyze, interpret, and judge dances, as well as to make specific suggestions to contribute to choreographers' development of their works-in-progress, the ORDER approach fosters substantive critical discourse along with a clear understanding of the terms and concepts employed in that discourse.

In learning to use the ORDER approach, some readers will encounter the philosophical and practical issues surrounding critical evaluation in art for the first time. These readers will discover that critical evaluation is not something that only "experts" can do. Instead, readers will learn to do it themselves, and in so doing will gain confidence as dance artists.

For those readers who are already experienced in dance-making and talking about dances and other works of art, this book will provide new insights into the way critical evaluation—when done well—can actually help artists to understand and improve their work and appreciate the artistic efforts of others. Young writers of dance criticism will find that the ORDER approach sharpens their skills in looking, seeing, and evaluating, helping them to write more thorough and clearly articulated reviews.

The ORDER Approach Facilitates Critical Thinking Skills

The ORDER approach strongly emphasizes careful observation, and it focuses attention on personal reflection and note taking that lead to verbal description, analysis, interpretation, and judgment of a dance. It does these things by directing critical attention to the ways the perceptual experience of each viewer is affected by the dance's *visible features*. Because of this emphasis on the visible features of the work under review, the ORDER approach can be called a *phenomenological method* for conducting critical evaluation. Phenomenology focuses on describing and understanding an experience *the way it occurred*, rather than influences upon, hypotheses about, or theories of that experience. Since phenomenology stresses concentrated observation and personal reflection upon one's experiences, it forms the basis of this new approach to observing and discussing the dances one sees.

The ORDER approach hones students' skills in analyzing what they see and in learning to formulate and recognize substantive arguments. These skills are essential to students' development both as creative artists and in other fields in which they study or work. Developing such reasoning skills is also known as the practice of critical thinking. This practice is described by Joanne G. Kurfiss (1988) as "an investigation whose purpose is to explore a situation, phenomenon, question, or problem, to arrive at a hypothesis or conclusion about it that integrates all available information and that can therefore be convincingly justified" (p.2).

Discovery and Justification: Two Essential Components

Two essential components of critical thinking skills development, identified by Kurfiss and others as important to all educational domains, are features of the ORDER approach. These are *discovery* and *justification*. During the discovery phase, evidence is observed, reviewed, and assessed. The justification phase involves the presentation and defense of an argument. In the ORDER approach, the observation of a dance, reflection on the experience of having seen the dance, and the verbal sharing of one's reflective description and analysis of the dance correspond to the discovery phase of critical inquiry. Volunteering interpretations, judgments, and recommendations for revisions, as well as debating the merits of these, correspond to the justification phase.

Taken as a whole, then, the ORDER approach systematically introduces into the choreography course essential components of the practice of critical thinking. In so doing, it proposes that the classroom environment is a model of the larger critical community (consisting of professional artists, critics, writers, designers, producers, and arts advocates) that the students will eventually enter, where they expect to be able to make a meaningful contribution.

Critical Writing: A Reflective Component

A key element of the ORDER approach is the reflective writing stage, a precursor to the group discussion stage. Group conversations do develop students' abilities to listen and respond quickly and coherently to others' views. But the practice of writing, because it is a more reflective process than speaking, stimulates even greater perceptiveness and clarity of thought than impromptu discussion. This is because the act of writing involves three separate modes of learning: doing, seeing, and verbalizing. Thus, in order to focus students' reflective attention upon the structures and dynamic relationships of each work seen, a reflective writing step precedes discussion of students' reactions to each dance.

How This Book Is Organized

For purposes of clarity, I have divided the entire critical process into separate stages and aspects. It is important to note that, in actual practice, critical evaluation is a more fluid, seamless process than this or any other analytical account of it may suggest. Readers should feel free to adapt the ideas presented here to their specific teaching and learning situations.

The five chapters in Part I provide an overview of philosophical and pedagogical issues and perspectives on critical evaluation and its role in dance educational settings. The discussion identifies the five "Teaching/Learning Principles" upon which the ORDER approach is based. As an aid to thinking and discussion, there are "Think on It" prompts for further reflection and writing included throughout the text.

In Part II the ORDER approach to critical evaluation is outlined. A separate chapter is devoted to explaining each step in the approach—Observation, Reflection, Discussion, Evaluation, and Recommendations for revisions. More "Think on It" prompts for further reflection and writing are included in Part II to stimulate expanded thinking among teachers and students about the critical process and how it works. A number of "Teaching Hints" are included to help choreography teachers implement the ORDER approach in their classes.

In Part III, more practical suggestions for implementing the ORDER approach in beginning- and advanced-level choreography classes are provided, and the theoretical bases for these suggestions is explained. The interweaving of practical and theoretical considerations will be useful for teachers and students alike who seek to understand the relationship between the philosophy of criticism and critical practice.

Experienced teachers and choreographers will benefit from reading the chapters in sequence. However, newer choreographers grappling for the first time with the challenges of dance-making and discussing dances may find it useful to begin with Part II, where the steps of the ORDER approach to critical evaluation are laid out in detail. Later, with the steps of the ORDER approach firmly in mind, it will be helpful to these readers to study the earlier chapters as well as the implementation chapters in Part III.

For all readers, I recommend returning to the text periodically, as this will provide greater perspectives on, and clarity of, the information it contains and the interrelated concepts it presents.

PART I

Perspectives on Critical Evaluation in Dance Education

A choreography class is a special place where teachers and students gather to explore the nature of dance and the visual and expressive power of human movement. Through the use of creative problem-solving experiments, choreography teachers lead their students to new discoveries about how dances are created. The choreography class is the laboratory where young artists usher in the dance of tomorrow, imbuing their works with the unique flavors, tones, and sensibilities of their time.

But more than just dancing must take place in the choreography class. For choreography students to develop all of the skills they need to function in an artistic community, focused critical talk about dance must happen as well. This critical dance talk must describe, analyze, interpret, evaluate, and recommend revisions for the works created and shared in class.

Dance students' enthusiasm for dance talk makes them perfectly suited for the kind of focused thinking about dance that is the ORDER approach to critical evaluation. This approach helps students learn how to observe carefully, describe accurately, analyze rationally, and support their interpretations and aesthetic judgments with reasons rather than emotions. In short, it teaches them to formulate clear and reasonable critical responses to dances they see, make, and perform.

In the five chapters of Part I, we will explore different perspectives on critical evaluation and its role in the choreography class. We will also correct a number of common myths about critical evaluation that both teachers and students believe, and introduce five "Teaching/Learning Principles" for critical evaluation.

The discussion in Part I will provide you with the framework of understanding you will need to successfully employ the ORDER approach to critical evaluation.

Chapter 1

CRITICISM WITHIN THE CHOREOGRAPHY CLASS

This chapter will help you understand

- the importance of substantive critical evaluation,
- the difference between casual dance talk and critical evaluation,
- the nature of the choreographic process, and
- the similarities between a choreography class and the larger art world.

The term *critical evaluation*, or criticism, provokes varied reactions among dance educators. Some believe it threatens a permissive educational environment, while others embrace it as essential to students' artistic growth. Teachers rarely agree on how much class time and effort should be devoted to critical discussion, and many only tentatively acknowledge the important role substantive criticism can play in students' creative efforts.

The reluctance many teachers have to devote time and effort to effective critical evaluation can lead to frustration for students. Consider the following scenario: Lisa has just performed a short dance and is awaiting the responses of her classmates. Several viewers immediately voice their first impressions of the work. One student says Lisa's piece reminded her of a sad situation in her life. Another says he thinks the dance still needs some work, but he found it exciting. A third reports that he liked the dance but would really like to know what Lisa intended it to mean.

Hearing these comments, Lisa is gratified that her colleagues seem pleased with her work, but she also notices that the comments primarily reflect the students' *feelings* in response to the dance. The third student even made it clear that, in forming his opinion, he valued Lisa's interpretation over his own reaction. But none of the students' comments focused on any specific aspect of the dance itself—the movements, the choreographic structure, or even her performance. In short, the responses provided Lisa with no substantive feedback on the qualities of her dance. She leaves class thinking that somehow she missed out on something that she might have gotten from the class.

Lisa's experience illustrates a common fact about many choreography classes: While considerable time is devoted to discussing students' work, helping novice choreographers refine their creative products is addressed only marginally at best. For students' responses to each other's work to develop beyond descriptions of their feelings, they must learn the difference between critical evaluation and casual conversation. As well, they need a choreography curriculum that fully integrates training in the theory and practice of critical evaluation.

Many choreography teachers do not believe they can fit substantive critical evaluation into the class time available in their courses. After all, many see dance as a physical, not a verbal, art and take for granted that students need to work exclusively on improvising, exploring, and practicing movement, experimenting with as many creative methods and devices as possible. Developing students' competence in critical evaluation might seem like a worthwhile ideal, but, for many dance instructors, finding a way to incorporate it into the choreography class seems an overwhelming challenge. This has reinforced the myth of the nonintellectual dancer: the notion that the kind of person drawn to dance is ill equipped to engage in serious critical discussion. This myth pervades many choreography classes where teachers consider it sufficient that students *do* dance, and have no motivation to analyze or assess dancing and choreography.

THINK ON IT
Ideas for Writing and Discussion

How do you perceive the relationship between making dances and evaluating them? Are there any skills that are involved in both? What are they? How does your own process of making dances involve your critical mind?

Casual Conversation and Critical Discourse

Dance students, particularly at the college level, are rarely satisfied merely to do dance—they also want to discuss it, and they attempt to critique dances extensively among themselves. They talk about dances they have seen, read about, or performed in; they talk about performances, challenge and support each other's views, and exchange ideas about the nature of dance. This dance talk occurs before and after performances as well as while dances are being created (in and out of class) and rehearsed.

What dance students and teachers may not realize is that casual conversations about dance differ dramatically from formal critical discourse. Indeed, casual conversation and critical evaluation are two distinct categories of talk, with highly individualized, specific purposes and forms.

Casual conversation tends to shift focus rapidly and often, leaving the ideas and themes of one moment forgotten in the next. Casual conversation primarily aims at airing initial reactions and opinions, not at delivering rigorously formulated, substantiated views. Critical discussion, on the other hand, functions both as a mode of *reflective inquiry* and as a mode of *persuasion*. It proceeds systematically through a series of simple steps, from general to specific statements about the work under review. If you analyzed a sample of casual dance talk among students, you would no doubt find mixed into it the rough equivalents of several elements of critical discourse—for example, there would probably be descriptions, theoretical speculations, and perhaps even initial hypotheses of interpretation. But it is highly unlikely that these elements would function in the disciplined, directed way they do in critical discourse. Dance students are like other people: They converse easily, but they practice critical evaluation rather poorly—unless they have deliberate instruction in how it is done.

Consider the following conversation among three students, following observation of a dance:

> **Bill:** *"Wow, that music was terrific. I have to find out what it is. Maybe I could use something like that in my next piece."*
>
> **Ellen:** *"Those skirts were too long, but I liked the colors. I would have liked to see the dancers' bodies more clearly. I wonder why the women had their hair up."*
>
> **Felix:** *"The last time I saw a dance concert, I was just getting over the flu, and it made me dizzy to watch the fast sections. This piece was mostly slow."*

Conversations of this kind are typical and foster camaraderie among the students. However, they are not conversations in which students actually respond to—much less seek elaboration upon—the remarks made by others, and the remarks say very little about the dance. While Bill, Ellen, and Felix have each given a preliminary response of sorts to the dance, their conversation was not in any sense a critical discussion, nor did it utilize or develop any critical skills.

A critical discussion of the same dance among Bill, Ellen, and Felix might begin like this:

Bill: *"I noticed a rhythmic relationship between the music and the choreography. Sometimes the dancers were with the rhythm of the music, but sometimes they were not."*

Ellen: *"That's really true. Did you see how first one and then the other dancer moved out of sync with the music, but then they moved back with the music at the same time? There was a real sense of unity between the two of them at that point."*

Felix: *"I think that is what the whole piece was about, actually— the way the two dancers, who at first were a bit antagonistic toward each other, got together. By bringing them together rhythmically, the theme of the dance showed very well in its structure."*

In this discussion, visible aspects of the dance are described, and their contribution to the dance's meaning are assessed. Bill's opening comments about the relationship between the movement and the music are elaborated on by Ellen. Then Felix offers a preliminary interpretation and judgment of the work that incorporates Bill's and Ellen's analyses.

It is important for students not only to talk to each other in the casual manner typified by the first conversation, but also to know how to use an approach geared toward systematic investigation of a work of art. Moreover, since student choreographers engaging in critical evaluation are often asked to offer suggestions for revision to their student colleagues, their evaluative talk needs to be geared toward formulation of cogent and precise feedback. For the choreographer, the second conversation would be far more useful to hear than the first.

THINK ON IT
Ideas for Writing and Discussion

Critical talk about dance takes place in all kinds of settings: before, during, and after classes and rehearsals, during intermission, and following performances. What kinds of remarks do you usually make when you engage in dance talk? Do you talk about movement combinations? qualities of a particular dancer's performance? the differences and similarities among different styles of dance? How does this kind of talk affect your work as a performer or choreographer?

Choreography Is a Revisions Process

Making dances, like any creative process, essentially consists of putting something together using the materials of the art form—in this case, movements—and then assessing the piece, taking it apart, and putting it together again, likely with some changes. Pablo Picasso often described his painting process in the same way. Looking at the choreographic process in this manner highlights the fact that critical evaluation focusing on aspects of the work itself—that is, *substantive* critical evaluation—plays a pivotal role throughout the process of creating a work of art. For in making a dance, choreographers are always their own first evaluators, as they inevitably try out ideas; stop along the way to analyze, interpret, and assess the way the work is coming together; and erase, revise, and switch directions a few times before arriving at a "finished" dance composition.

In the educational setting, when this kind of focused self-evaluation is supplemented by thoughtful and reasoned feedback from teachers and peers, it helps the student choreographer to avoid *premature closure*—declaring a piece finished for lack of further ideas on how to develop or refine it. With the aid of substantive feedback from teachers and peers, the artist can instead persist in exploring alternative solutions to the various creative problems inherent in the making of every dance. But the only feedback that will benefit the student artist is that which directly addresses specific, visible features of the work under review. If the critical response is primarily a report on how the observer felt after viewing the work, the evaluation process is not useful to the artist. In such situations, student choreographers are left with little to go on.

The Creator as Critic

A revision process in any of the arts involves frequent assessment and adjustment of a work-in-progress. In the initial stages, these assessments are made by creators. Many students first learn revision skills in their English composition and foreign language courses. In both these disciplines, the creative process of writing entails repeated self-reviews and evaluations of the work-in-progress. By studying the revision process in the choreography class, educators and students can explore something that has generally been left unstudied in our discipline: the tension between the creative and the critical *I*'s of the artist. Dancers typically experience this tension as a dialogue between two inner voices: the voice of the *I* who is creating the movements, patterns, and structures of the dance, and the voice of the *I* who is assessing the unfolding composition. As any choreographer can attest, these two voices are not always in harmony: The creator might find the voice of the evaluator harsh and judgmental, while the evaluator often suspects the creator of being incompetent or lazy.

The Dialogue Between the Artist and the Materials of Art

In addition to the dialogue between an artist's critical and creative voices, a second kind of dialogue takes place during the creative process between the choreographer and the *materials* of dance—the totality of the possibilities of movement. This dialogue begins for student choreographers when they start to discover the limitations of movement and learn how the individual components of movement mutually affect each other. For example, in a study of body shape, the novice choreographer may discover how one series of changes in shape restricts the movement of the body in space, while other changes propel the body through space. Later, in a study of floor patterns, the choreographer may see how a dancer's speed can limit the ability to make sharp directional changes and to maintain the integrity of body shapes while moving along the selected path. The many choices and adjustments choreographers make as they encounter such possibilities and limitations constitute their dialogue with the materials of dance.

The Nature of Artistic Creativity

It is crucial for students and teachers of choreography to understand not only that artistic creativity necessarily involves the dialogues just discussed, but also that choreographers and dancers often perceive these dialogues as struggles. To make dances, artists must persevere in the face of these struggles.

Often, students assume that art-making will, or should, be easy—that it is simply a spontaneous process of expressing oneself. They may try to bypass the artist's struggle by imitating in their works the familiar patterns (of movement vocabulary, phrasing, and form) of other dances. Particularly at the beginning level, artists need frequent reminders that an authentic composition process usually necessitates experiencing struggle.

THINK ON IT
Ideas for Writing and Discussion

What is the creative process like for you? Is the dialogue between your critical mind and creative mind friendly or antagonistic? Is it easy or difficult for you to continue when the work is not going as you would like? What do you need to do to overcome obstacles that prevent you from enjoying the creative process?

The Idealist Notion of Creativity

Understanding that any creative process is a revision process demonstrates the fallacy of a misconception called the *idealist notion* that students often bring with them to the choreography class.

The idealist notion suggests that a work of art already exists in full form in the artist's mind and that the artist possesses a complete idea of the content to be expressed even before beginning to work. The work the artist does, then, is to adopt or construct an appropriate form for expression of the idea.

Accordingly, the finished work is assumed to somehow fully represent predetermined meanings that existed beforehand in pure form in the artist's mind. Working backwards, then, the viewer is expected to resynthesize the artist's original meaning from observing the physical aspects of the work.

Holding the idealist view can pose grave problems for choreography students. First, it often prevents them from beginning to explore movement, because they think they need to know what they want to "say" through their dances before starting. More important, it frequently leads them to assume that critical evaluation is nothing more than assessing the clarity with which a dance represented a choreographer's "meaning." Not surprisingly, when they present their own dances to the class, students who hold the idealist notion are often surprised and discouraged to discover that other people's understanding of their dances never quite penetrates the movements and choreographic structures. For these students, it seems that viewers can never grasp the "meaning" the choreographer intended the dance to convey. When these students see their dances being interpreted and judged in different ways by various viewers, many fear that the choreographic process itself has only distorted what they were trying to "say" through the use of movement.

The problems created by the idealist notion present a crucial dilemma in choreography classes. How should dance composition be taught to students who, after experiencing the initial shock of the revision process and its results, want only to retreat from the exploration, risk-taking, and changes that inevitably accompany art-making? It is a key challenge for the choreography class to expose the fallacy behind the assumption that to compose necessarily means that the artist will successfully communicate a predetermined meaning.

The Experience of Art

Thinking of creativity in art as a revision process in which an artist discovers and weaves possible meanings into a work rather than transfers a fixed meaning to the work enables students to see that a work of art may provide observers with varying experiences and give rise to different interpretations and judgments. For this reason, watching or attending to a dance is not merely receiving a "message" from the work's maker. Because a dance can be said to express anything that is consistent with its visible features, watching a dance is only the first of several steps in the process of critically evaluating that work. Only after a dance has been carefully observed should viewers practice other critical skills, including reflective description and analysis of the dance's visible features. Exercise of these skills allows students to formulate reasoned interpretations and justifications of their aesthetic judgments of the dance.

THINK ON IT
Ideas for Writing and Discussion

Have you ever thought that a dance already exists fully formed in an artist's mind before he or she creates the movements of the work? What do you think of that idea? How and when did you develop your perspective? In what ways do you see your perspective helping or hindering your creative process?

The Choreography Classroom as an Art World

As we go on to explore the role of substantive critical evaluation in the process of making dances, it is useful to think of the choreography class as a miniature *art world*. The art world is one in which there are no universal or permanent standards of judgment and no guarantees of critical agreement. Instead, one finds many competing ideas about artistic meaning and about what constitutes "good" art. In the choreography class, students reflect on their own descriptions and analyses of the dances they observe. These personal reflections lead to the formulation of various interpretations and judgments of dances and to the discussion of these views with other people.

As discussion proceeds in the art world of the choreography class, students who tend to agree with each other informally cluster into *critical alliances* within the group as a whole. During each discussion, the viewpoint of one of these critical alliances may seem for the moment to prevail over others. One perspective may, for example, deal most thoroughly and persuasively with the visible features of the work under review. But it is here that critical discourse is most unlike informal conversations or even arguments between people: The objective is never for one "side" to "win" the discussion. Instead, in the context of an art world, the views of one critical alliance hold center stage only temporarily. Others remain on the fringe, but only until their viewpoints emerge, perhaps in evaluating the next dance observed, and become dominant.

As choreography students continue to make and discuss dances that raise new and different aesthetic issues, they generate new perspectives on familiar questions. New critical alliances continuously take shape. This causes ever-shifting alignments within the class or art world. The ORDER approach to formulating critical responses is ideally suited to this dynamic process, allowing students to develop and articulate their own standards of artistic judgment.

Summary: Important Points to Remember

1. Casual dance talk and critical evaluation are two distinct categories of discussion. Casual conversations tend to shift focus rapidly while critical evaluation proceeds systematically from general to specific statements about a particular work.

2. Choreography, like other art-making activities, is a revision process consisting of putting something together, assessing it, taking it apart, and putting it together again, often many times over.

3. The choreography class is a miniature art world in which there are many different ideas about artistic meaning and about what constitutes "good" art. In the choreography class, students align themselves into smaller critical alliances in accordance with their critical perspectives on the dances they see and evaluate.

Chapter 2

THE
SUBJECTIVE
RESPONSE

This chapter will help you understand

- the difference between an emotional response to a dance and a critical evaluation of it,
- the pitfalls of subjectivist reasoning, and
- the role of feelings in the critical process.

Immediately after watching a dance, we are usually strongly aware of the feelings the experience aroused in us. Our first inclination, then, is to talk about whether or not we "liked" the work, the way students in Lisa's choreography class did (chapter 1). When we are asked to verbalize any additional reactions to the piece, we still generally find ourselves talking at length about our feelings, saying little about the dance itself.

Viewers' initial *emotional* reactions to a piece are generally intense and tend to dominate their evaluations of the work. It should come as no surprise, then, that this initial emotional intensity leads some evaluators to believe that giving their emotional response is equivalent to evaluating a dance. In other words, evaluation is thought by some to consist of statements about whether or not a work was pleasing to behold. This kind of reaction is called the *subjective response*, and the belief that the subjective "I liked it" statement is a valid critical response is called the *subjectivist approach*.

Advocates for the subjectivist approach argue that critical evaluation is based on each person's individual taste. But giving a subjective response is actually very different from offering a critical reaction, just as an audience member at a performance is different from a critic viewing the work. These distinctions have important implications for the choreography class, because they imply different responsibilities for students as they view each other's work.

Subjectivity and the Viewer's Role as Audience Member

The term *audience member* generally refers to any observer who, in the words of art educator Howard Gardner (1973), "experiences feelings in relationship to his perception of an art object" (p. 326). By contrast, the term *critic* refers to someone who has

- a special knowledge of the art form in general and

- a particular ability to formulate, weigh, and assess competing interpretations and judgments of the work under review.

Too often in choreography classes students function merely as audience members when they view dances. This happens for three reasons. The first is that most students have never viewed art in any other way because they do not have critical-evaluation skills. Second, teachers may never have learned the difference between being the "feeling" recipient or audience member that Gardner describes and the possibilities viewers have for producing other levels of reaction.

The third reason for students remaining in the role of audience members, however, is the most compelling for teachers: Very simply, it just seems to be the easiest way to ensure that all students participate in class discussion. For if any feelings experienced by a viewer are treated as appropriate critical evaluation, then even shy or inexperienced observers feel more comfortable volunteering comments in class. Teachers commonly assume that shy students are encouraged by the fact that discussing personal feelings tends to be less rigorous and less likely to provoke disagreements than more systematic analyses of observations about concrete, visible aspects of a dance.

So teachers are often seduced by the ease of the subjectivist approach to responding to works of art. They neglect to focus class discussions on visible features of the dance itself, which would turn audience members into critics (even if only for a short while). This omission is a disservice to the students who expect their educational experiences viewing dances to elevate their levels of reaction beyond those of a casual observer who may never even have seen a dance before. And it is a particular disservice to student choreographers, because it deprives them of the chance to learn which aspects of their dances have elicited interpretations and judgments from viewers. For their peers to be confined to the role of mere audience members leaves student choreographers with the uncomfortable impression that their artistic endeavors are going to be judged solely on the basis of other people's claimed experiences of happiness, boredom, or some other emotion while observing the work.

The Nature of the Subjectivist Approach

The first question asked following the performance of a dance in many choreography classes is often "Well—did you like it?" This question generally triggers a discussion of viewers' feelings about the dance rather than statements relating to specific aspects of the piece.

The notion that "Did you like it?" is the most crucial question to ask following observation of a work of art is strongly endorsed by many dance educators. Jacqueline M. Smith (1976, 93–98), for example, after listing over 50 interesting questions one can ask about a dance— concerning such things as movement, actions, space, and staging— concludes that the fundamental standard for judging art is "pleasure." She asserts that "Did you like it" is "the most important question to ask" about a work of art .

The subjectivist approach, then, defines artistic value exclusively in terms of the viewer's emotional response to the work. As what might be called the "pleasure theory" of critical evaluation, it essentially equates artistic success with popular success. In the subjectivist approach, all critical judgments are expressions of arbitrary, intuitive preferences.

But subjectivism is based on a set of assumptions that themselves rest on a central misconception. First is the assumption that liking a work of art is the same as obtaining from it feelings of pleasure. The corollary of this assumption is that disliking a work of art is the same as reacting with feelings of displeasure. These correspondences may indeed be experienced by some viewers. But other viewers may admire and approve of—i.e., like—works that also arouse in them feelings of displeasure or disgust. Or they may dislike and disapprove of works that stimulate pleasant feelings.

A second fallacy of the subjectivist approach is the assumption that all works of art provoke feelings of pleasure or displeasure. In fact, some works of art provoke only intellectual responses, arousing no emotion-based reactions at all.

Finally, regardless of whether liking or disliking directly corresponds with pleasure or displeasure, liking a work and judging it are nevertheless two different concepts. Likes and dislikes are personal feelings, while judgments are not feelings at all. A judgment is the culmination of a systematic process of concentrated reflection upon a subject. In other words, we *have* likings, but we *arrive at* judgments. Of course, a person who judges a work may also happen to like or dislike it. But liking and judging do not both always occur, and even if they do, likings cannot be the basis of judgments we arrive at through reflection on various aspects of the work.

THINK ON IT
Ideas for Writing and Discussion

Have you ever found yourself liking a work of art—say, a book, a movie, or a dance—even though you also considered it a poor piece of work? Have you ever found yourself not liking, or feeling indifferent toward, a work of art that you knew was considered by many to be a great work? How would you explain this?

Confusion About Feelings in Art

In addition to confusing the relationship between liking or disliking and genuine critical assessment, the subjectivist viewpoint gives high priority to emotions that may be associated with a work of art. This leads to further confusion between emotions felt by a viewer and those supposedly expressed by the work of art.

There is an important distinction between the emotions one person feels and those a work of art or another person may (or may not) be expressing. Consider, for example, that when one person expresses anger, the other might respond by feeling fear. When someone expresses grief, the other person might react with a feeling of empathy. It is essential to remember that the emotions a viewer feels are not necessarily the same as those being expressed by a performer or by a work. So a viewer who says, "I don't like that dance because it is gloomy," may only be saying that she or he dislikes the feeling of being gloomy. The error is in failing to distinguish between one's awareness of a work of art that contains emotions and the experience of emotions within oneself.

The Pitfalls of Subjectivist Reasoning

The logic of subjectivism breaks down when one pursues three common situations to their conclusions from a subjectivist point of view. The first occurs when a work of art is at once liked by some and despised by others. The second happens when a work arouses no particular reaction in anyone. The third concerns a work a viewer initially dislikes but eventually likes.

In these three situations, the logic of subjectivism inevitably leads to the following conclusions:

1. Works of art that some people despise but others adore must be both excellent and poor.
2. Works of art that arouse no emotions cannot be evaluated at all.
3. Works that were disliked before but are now loved must have been poor at one time, but have somehow managed to become excellent.

The absurdity of these conclusions reveals the central error upon which the subjectivist approach is based: that feeling-based responses can serve as a basis for judgment. This proposition fails because there is no clear relationship between a feeling response and the work under review. The student in Lisa's class (chapter 1) who stated that Lisa's dance made her feel sad may have had sad feelings before the dance began. In any case, this student's account of her emotions makes no comment on the merit of the dance under review.

Genuine critical evaluation requires, therefore, that the visible features of a work of art be the focus of consideration, and that viewers learn to move beyond their feelings to assess, instead, the dance they saw. Dance theorist and educator Pauline Hodgens (1988, 94) puts it this way:

> *The evaluation of any dance which rests upon experiential values can only be valid or worth consideration if the experience cited relates directly to the dance. Although the evaluation will be "personal" in the sense that it has to do with how the individual experiences the dance . . . the reasons for the experience, opinion and judgement are found in the features, forms, characters, qualities, meanings or significance of the dance itself.*

Overcoming Subjectivism: The Essential Question to Ask

We can see that the essential question of critical evaluation cannot be "Did you like it?" Rather, the question that should be posed to students following the performance of a dance is "What did you see in the dance?" This question solicits descriptive statements specifically about the dance, not accounts of the feelings of the viewers. Descriptive statements launch critical discussions that help choreographers learn what specific strengths and weaknesses viewers perceived in their dances. Descriptions can be elaborated upon, checked for relevance to the work itself, and used as the basis for interpretations and judgments of the dance. Reports of feelings, on the other hand, cannot stimulate further discussion of the properties of a dance.

The Role of Subjectivity in the Critical Process

A consideration of the distinction between the audience member and the critic as well as the problems inherent in a subjective evaluation of art prompts the questions, "Just how relevant is the feeling-based response of the viewer to critical evaluation? What is the proper place of subjectivity in the critical process?" These questions are, of course, central to all critical theories. They do need to be con-sidered when thinking about how to teach students critical skills.

The relationship between feeling-based responses and critical evaluation can be highlighted as part of the effort to steer critical discussions toward the formulation of descriptive and analytical statements about dances. Students can preface their critical remarks by volunteering whatever feelings the work under review has provoked in them. In fact, teachers should build on these initial feeling-based responses by encouraging students to consider which aspects of the dance triggered the feelings.

Putting subjective responses and critical observation in their proper places will enable students to correlate their feeling-based responses with visible aspects of the dance under review. They will then be able to turn their attention to the forms and features of the dance as they formulate authentic critical reactions to the work. In short, students will discover that aesthetic judgments are more than statements of subjective feelings. Aesthetic judgments are objective in nature because they are based on rational observations. Thus, the first principle upon which the ORDER approach to critical evaluation is based is as follows:

Teaching/Learning Principle

Subjective, or feeling-based, responses can play only a preliminary role in the critical response, and they must not be considered a sufficient basis for making aesthetic judgments because they describe the viewer rather than the dance under review.

Summary: Important Points to Remember

1. For genuine critical evaluation to take place in the choreography class, students must learn to move beyond the subjective or feeling-based response to the dance under review.

2. While viewers' initial emotional reactions to a dance may be intense, a genuine critical response is more than the articulation of one's feelings about the work under review. Liking and judging a work of art are two different things. One has likings, but one arrives at judgments through reflection.

3. It is perfectly valid to preface critical remarks with feeling responses. But evaluators should build upon these initial remarks by describing which aspects of the dance triggered the feelings. This will enable them to correlate feeling-based responses with visible aspects of the dance under review.

Chapter 3

THE PROBLEM OF USING PREDETERMINED CRITERIA

This chapter will help you understand

- how "rules" for judging works of art stifle the critical process before it has even begun,
- how critical standards are continually changing, and
- how different theories of art and dance give rise to different critical standards.

Many students recognize the need to go beyond "Did you like it?" in critical evaluation. In their attempt to escape the kind of subjectivism discussed in chapter 2, however, they often turn to an expert to receive a precise list from on high of things to look for in evaluating a work of art. In an effort to provide students with structure, some dance educators give their students lists of predetermined rules, or *criteria*, for judging other students' dances. In this chapter we will consider whether this strategy is useful for fostering substantive critical evaluation.

The Risks of Predetermined Criteria

A list of art principles may seem, at first glance, a reasonably objective (as opposed to subjective) basis for the critical evaluation of dances. But it has the drawback of preventing students from developing and articulating their own artistic values. Instead, predetermined criteria lead students to translate their own experiences of the work into the words of the criteria provided by the teacher.

Typically, the criteria provided in choreography classes turn out to be generalizations from the personal artistic preferences of the teacher. So instead of moving the practices of dance-making and critical evaluation beyond arbitrary personal preferences, the use of predetermined criteria can actually have the effect of setting in concrete a teacher's own (perhaps unexamined) artistic assumptions. Using such lists only undermines rigorous critical debate in the classroom because it sets up a kind of false objectivity. As a result, students often overlook features of the work under review that do not match what they have been told to look for in dances.

Yet choreography teachers who stipulate predetermined criteria for evaluation might argue that such standards save critical discourse from the chaos that might ensue if all artistic standards were considered equally acceptable. These teachers contend that if any standard whatever is acceptable, students cannot practice critical skills because one must establish what is and is not "good" art before trying to evaluate a work. Underlying this point of view are two powerful but misleading assumptions:

1. Some fixed set of objective artistic standards in fact exists.
2. One must accept the authority of these standards in order to discuss works of art.

Can Objective Standards Exist?

The first assumption fails to recognize that within the art community—the world of artists, critics, designers, producers, collectors, scholars, and all other arts professionals and advocates—there is no single fixed standard of artistic judgment. Instead, there are many critical alliances, each with a viewpoint different from the others. At any given time, any of these viewpoints may be central within the art world, but only temporarily, because other viewpoints are always competing to become the most widely accepted. Even so, wide acceptance merely indicates a new temporary alignment of values in which other critical alliances occupy positions on the fringe for the time being.

Acceptability in the art community, therefore, is continually being established and reestablished. And the notions of acceptability and unacceptability depend upon one another for meaning: knowing what is currently acceptable implies that one automatically knows what is not.

Like the art community in general, a choreography class in which the students are taught systematically to reflect on and discuss dances contains many different critical positions. As the students identify and debate various aesthetic issues, several critical viewpoints naturally emerge—critical discourse can operate in no other way. By its very nature, critical discourse consists of constant negotiation over artistic values among all those who join in the debate over the interpretation and judgment of works of art. There is never a time when all artistic standards are equally acceptable to the group. In any discussion in which one critical position emerges as the most acceptable, the alternative positions necessarily become less acceptable.

This reality of critical debate actually relieves teachers of the need to provide fixed or absolute criteria for judging dances. There is no threat of a chaos of different and equally acceptable viewpoints because, in true critical discourse, various views are continually gaining and losing acceptability.

The Educational Hazards of Accepting Fixed Standards

A second assumption is that to be able to critique works of art students must accept the authority of conventional standards of artistic excellence. But we have seen that no single set of artistic standards holds a fixed position of authority. Therefore, to press upon students prevailing critical standards actually teaches them nothing about how to discover the ways art influences our perceptions or about the fundamental nature of critical discourse. In fact, adopting a fixed set of standards may leave students unable to participate successfully in the ongoing cultural debate over critical standards.

Thus, all the participants in a choreography class should try to demonstrate the merits of their perceptions of each dance, but teachers should not promote any list of artistic principles as true or correct. A classroom is a special kind of (critical) community. No matter how innovative the course is, in the classroom a single member (the teacher) inevitably occupies a position of authority over the others (the students). This means that while it is appropriate for teachers to *inform* students of the prevailing or traditional standards of artistic excellence, setting forth any standards as being correct or absolute takes unfair advantage of the teacher's position in the class.

Perhaps more important, a teacher who provides a list of standards exempts those standards from the test of relevance to the dance under review. Moreover, lists of criteria tend to silence students who might propose (either in discussion or through their creative works) different artistic values. Thus, the use of fixed standards of artistic value exerts an unfortunate chilling effect on creativity and stifles critical discourse in the classroom.

THINK ON IT
Ideas for Writing and Discussion

Think back to when you first became interested in dance. What criteria or standards did you use then to evaluate dances? Do you still evaluate dances according to the same standards? In what ways have your ideas of what makes a good dance changed? What has caused these changes?

The Risks of Theory-Based Criteria

Despite the risks to learning we just discussed, it is tempting for choreography teachers to evaluate students' dances based on a single theory of art or dance. For example, a common basis of some teachers' approaches to dance composition and evaluation is *communication theory*. Esther Pease (1966) reflected this theory when she wrote that dance "is meant to be looked at in terms of its communication—if its meaning is unclear or its purpose does not come across, then the creator tries harder next time" (p. 24).

The problem with teaching approaches based on theories is that they state as facts the assumptions governing their particular theories. These assumptions, in turn, imply or lead explicitly to a predetermined way of judging dances. For example, Pease does not admit the possibility that a choreographer may create a work in which there is no intended meaning or "message." By themselves, then, theory-based principles of artistic value do not determine whether a dance can be considered mediocre or superb. In other words, the mere presence in a work of an attribute that happens to correspond with a particular theory does not make the work successful. Because each dance is different, an attribute like repetition, contrast, or any other general artistic value may improve some works while ruining others. Each work has to be evaluated on its own terms.

Compounding the Risks: Predetermined Discussion Questions

The common assumption that critical judgments should take the form of logical arguments often misleads choreography students into believing that there are ready-made formulas for creating good dance and for arriving at reasonable critical viewpoints. It implies that one need only learn and follow the "rules" to achieve success as an artist or critic. This problem is compounded when teachers offer not only predetermined criteria for judgment, but predetermined questions to guide critical evaluation as well. For example, a typical question posed to students after they have watched a dance is, "Is the intention of the choreographer communicated clearly?"

The danger in using predetermined questions as a substitute for critical discussion is that the artistic values within the questions tend to remain unexplored. The previous question, for example, implies that art is a form of direct communication of specific meaning from artist to audience. Moreover, the question suggests that successful communication of this meaning equals artistic success.

The notions that artists attach specific meanings to their works and that the aim of critical evaluation is to uncover and decode those meanings is widely debated among philosophers of art and criticism. But the various positions and ideas that inform this debate are not given the opportunity to emerge and be examined as students respond to the question, "Is the intention of the choreographer communicated clearly?" Instead, the question prompts premature "yes" or "no" judgments that speculate as to the nature of the message supposedly conveyed by the work. The assumptions in the question itself are left unidentified and unexplored.

Another pitfall of the teacher-led question-and-answer approach is that asking several questions successively tends to allow for only brief responses. These questions often depend entirely on short-term memory and contribute nothing to students' abilities to analyze, make interpretations, and arrive at reasoned judgments. In short, using question-and-answer strategies risks instilling in students a set of predetermined criteria.

Educators who stipulate predetermined values—whether these are embedded in questions or stated as facts about art—reduce critical evaluation to a rote process that pretends to be logical classification. If students count up the number of features a work has from some master list of features a work is "supposed" to have, it is possible for them to conclude that a dance having nine out of ten prescribed characteristics can be called "better" than a dance having only six. As mentioned earlier, the hazard of such an approach for students is that it radically devalues the individual's own perception of the work of art, making it secondary to formalized rules.

Carried to its extreme, the use of predetermined criteria may result in a viewer's feeling bound to agree that a particular work is excellent, when in fact he or she did not detect excellence in it at all. Indeed, one could even find oneself in the awkward position of saying "If I did not know that, according to the criteria I have been given for judging dances, this rates as a great work, I'd say it was quite poor." Clearly, there is no sound reason for teachers to place students in such a position. Therefore, the second principle upon which the ORDER approach is based is:

Teaching/Learning Principle

Critical judgments of a dance should not be based on predetermined criteria for artistic excellence. Instead, they should be guided by the visible features of the dance and the experience viewers have of those features and their relationships to each other.

Summary: Important Points to Remember

1. The use of predetermined criteria for judgment of dances or other works of art prevents students from developing and articulating their own artistic values.

2. There are no fixed or permanent standards for judging art. Instead, there are many critical alliances, each with a viewpoint different from the others. Therefore, what counts as "good" or "poor" art is continually being established and reestablished.

Chapter 4

THE PROBLEM OF RELYING ON ARTISTS' INTENTIONS

This chapter will help you understand

- the concept of intention as it relates to art-making,
- the fallacy of assuming that critical evaluation of a work depends on discovering the artist's intentions, and
- the concept of communication as it relates to art.

Immediately after seeing a dance, many viewers find that they don't understand what they have seen. They might turn to their neighbors and ask, "What was that all about? Did you understand what was going on in that dance?" It is tempting in such cases to look to a work's maker for an explanation of its "meaning." When this happens, the viewer is assuming that the work's true meaning is whatever the choreographer says it is. This assumption has been long debated in the philosophy of art. Looking for the artist's "intention" brings up a central question for the practice of critical evaluation: What relevance, if any, does consideration of an artist's intentions in a given work have to interpreting the meaning(s) or assessing the success of that work?

The search for the artist's intentions is a key element of communication and expression theories of art. But there is dispute over how to determine what an artist's intentions may have been and, further, over the value that knowing these might have for the critic.

The Concept of Intention

The term *intention* is ambiguous. It may refer either to the plan an artist has in mind while composing a work, or to the artist's own interpretation of the completed work. There is also a distinction between an artist's goals, or reasons for undertaking a certain project, and what the artist might be trying to do or say through the work of art. In short—comparing dance with speech for a moment — there is a difference between what one intends to accomplish by saying something and the definitions (or surface meanings) of the words one uses.

Communication and expression theories of dance tend to merge the two definitions of intention into one. They also rely heavily on the assumption that choreographers specifically try to communicate particular emotions and attitudes through movements. Expression theory as it applies to dance is explained by Mary Sirridge and Adina Armelagos (1977), who write:

The Expression Theory has been stronger in dance literature and criticism than perhaps anywhere else in the arts. On this theory, the performance is construed as a vehicle by which the dancer expresses his feelings, emotions, or attitudes in an attempt to engender these emotions or attitudes as a response in the audience. The human body, it is claimed, is the simplest and oldest medium for the communication of emotion and attitude. And that, it is claimed, is obviously what is going on in a dance performance. (p. 15)

Many people assume that a dancer's purpose is to arouse certain emotions in the spectator and that the movements the dancer performs must inevitably have literal or emotional connotations. A discussion in a choreography class based on this assumption typically poses to the choreographer such questions as "What were you trying to communicate or express?" and "What did you mean by . . . ?" Reactions to the choreographer's answers to such questions usually include such comments as "Well, I certainly did not get *that* meaning from the dance," or "Oh, now I see what you meant."

Underlying this kind of classroom exchange is the belief that because some artists create their works systematically, it must follow that each choreographer intends to express a particular idea that can be regarded as the actual or true meaning of the dance. In other words, there must be a fixed choreographic meaning that exists apart from the meaning viewers experience through the movements and structure of the piece. This fixed meaning supposedly existed in the choreographer's mind prior to the creative activity.

The danger in encouraging students to concern themselves with artists' intentions is that it undermines the notion of choreography as a process of revision during which the artist's initial aims are likely to be significantly transformed as the work-in-progress develops. Moreover, assigning priority to the artist's intention in a particular work causes the viewers to try to detect the artist's idea even while they are watching the work. As a result, the viewers' own immediate experience of the work's visible features and qualities may be sacrificed to the presumed past intentions of the artist. The viewer risks not truly seeing the work at all, because guessing at a meaning in the artist's mind prevents a genuine interaction with the work. Not surprisingly, it is easy for interpretation eventually to be seen as depending solely on the viewer's ability to find the artist's presumed intention in the work.

Looking for artists' intentions, then, tends to reduce critical evaluation to a kind of analytical decoding process. It also makes a "problem" out of the delightful ambiguity of many works of art and out of the way they take on various meanings simply through the interaction of their elements. Moreover, the search for intentions overlooks the fact that artists sometimes do not know, or are unable to explain, their intentions or the meanings of their works.

In the final analysis, a work of art as it has been experienced by the viewers is all there is to interpret or to judge. This means that even if a choreographer does explain, for example, that a particular dance was meant to be sadly ironic, unless the viewers themselves detect sad irony in the work, it cannot accurately be said to have been there. If knowledge of the choreographer's intention is ever relevant to critical evaluation, it is when such intentions are visible in the work itself. Thus, choreographers who, following a performance of their work, volunteer accounts of their intentions or interpretations must direct the critical attention of others to specific features of the work itself. And viewers should keep in mind that interpreting a dance solely on the basis of the choreographer's explanation of it or judging it solely by whether the viewers understood the choreographer's presumed intended meaning is not really evaluating the dance at all.

THINK ON IT
Ideas for Writing and Discussion

Have you ever started to create a work of art and been surprised to discover how it turned out as you worked on it? How did you proceed in creating that work? How did that experience differ from one in which you thought you knew exactly what you wanted to create before you started, and you stuck to that plan all the way through?

Communication and Dance

Despite the hazards involved in looking for artist's intentions, the notion persists that dance should inevitably be seen as *communication.* And somehow, the composer of a work is generally considered the best person to explain to others the work's true "message." Philosopher David Best (1978) explores this concept of communication and makes a distinction that helps dispel the notion that dance is a mode of communication. Best distinguishes between two kinds of communication, what he calls *linguistic* and *perceptual* communication (pp. 138-139).

Linguistic Communication

Best points out that in order for linguistic communication, or "lingcom," to take place between two people, the first—Jill—must understand what the second—Jack—does or says in the same precise sense in which Jack does or says it. There are criteria by which Jack can tell if he has communicated successfully. For example, if Jack says, "My brother has just arrived from New York," and Jill replies, "Yes, I would like some water," then Jack is justified in concluding that Jill has not understood what he said. Linguistic communication has not taken place.

Discussing dance, Best admits that it is not only possible, but quite common, for nonverbal behavior to result in communication in this lingcom sense. He writes:

> *For example, if you were standing on the opposite side of a swimming pool crowded with noisy bathers, and I wanted to communicate to you, despite my inability to shout above the hubbub, that the water was cold, I could grimace and perform simulated shivering movements. To take other obvious examples, a beckoning gesture, the hitch-hiker's thumbing sign, shaking a fist, and nodding the head, can communicate as effectively as saying the words "Come here," "May I have a lift," "I am angry with you," and "I agree." (p. 139)*

Here Best is pointing out that some movements do communicate in the lingcom sense—that is, a person can understand exactly what another intends to communicate through movements.

Perceptual Communication

Best also makes clear, however, that the majority of movements do not communicate in this sense. He describes another use of the term "communication" that is appropriate for cases in which Jack's movements communicate something he does not necessarily intend, or that is not necessarily true about him. For example, Jill might see Jack fidgeting in a doctor's waiting room. Jill might state, as a result, that Jack's movements communicated his anxiety. But Jack was not intending to communicate anything to anyone and may not have been anxious at all. The term "communication" can be used here only because Jill has perceived some feature of Jack's movement or behavior that she interprets as representing something. Best calls this perceptual communication, or *percom* (p. 140).

It is important to note that when the concept of communication in the percom sense is applied to movement, it can result only in the claim that all movement can be interpreted as a sign of something. Moreover, the belief that dances do, or should, communicate in a linguistic, or lingcom, sense—a belief assumed by the communication and expression theories of dance—is the result of confusing percom and lingcom.

As Best explains, the idea that all movement communicates perceptually is certainly true in the sense that all movement can be seen as suggesting one thing or another. But it is a mistake to leap from this truth to the conclusion that all movement communicates (or should communicate) linguistically. In order for a dance to communicate in the lingcom sense, it is necessary

1. for the dancer to intend to perform the specific movements in question (as opposed to improvising the movements), and also
2. for the choreographer to intend to communicate a particular meaning to the viewers.

Clearly, this double intention is not present in many dances. This is why it is a mistake for viewers to assume that choreographers can always explain the meaning of their works as if the movements in each dance were functioning the way words usually do.

THINK ON IT
Ideas for Writing and Discussion

Have you ever, after showing a dance to a group of friends or classmates, been pressed to explain the meaning of the work but found it difficult to do so? What did you say? Do you believe that artists should always be able, or required, to say what their works mean?

The Use of Intentions in Critical Evaluation

By discounting communication and expression theories of dance, it is easy to diminish the importance of questions about artists' intentions.

However, in an educational setting such as the choreography class, it is not necessary to avoid consideration of the artists' intentions in critical evaluation. Indeed, there may be a number of educational benefits for students in limited discussion with choreographers about their intentions in and interpretations of a particular dance. For example, to hear from a choreographer what principles of art or compositional strategies were used in crafting a dance teaches students how art practice might be informed by theory or how various concepts figure into the choreographic process.

But this is not to say that the choreographer's interpretation of the dance must be given priority over the interpretations of the viewers. In fact, often a choreographer will report that he or she did not intend to express a particular message or meaning through the dance. Hearing this helps student viewers learn that works of art have no single "correct" or "absolute" meaning and that to assume there is such a meaning—or that the artist can say precisely what it is—is a mistake. Even when a choreographer claims that the dance was intended to express one particular idea, often the choreographer's interpretation of the dance differs from that of one or more of the student viewers. Indeed, there may be several competing interpretations of a dance, each of which can be equally supported by the visible features of the work. Again, the important lesson is that there is no "correct" interpretation of a dance. Thus, the question for the class to consider in weighing competing interpretations is not "Who is the interpreter?" but "How well is the interpretation supported by the visible features of the work?"

Some student choreographers are disappointed when they discover that their intended meanings have not been perceived by the viewers. It is important, therefore, for teachers to convey two ideas to the class:

1. The aim of art-making is not necessarily to create works that are easy to understand or that communicate one precise message to all viewers.

2. The aim of critical discourse is not to achieve widespread agreement on what each work of art means.

In short, the ability of a dance to support many different interpretations is not a weakness. Instead, it is an indication of the work's richness and complexity, a point that is discussed further in chapter 8.

Some dances may immediately be "understood" by viewers and require no extended interpretive discussion. Other works may provoke no interpretive debate because they are perceived strictly as exercises in compositional design or structure or because they seem to be confused attempts to express some idea whose precise character is unclear. In such cases, the choreographer may attempt to explain the meaning of the work. But, as we have already discussed, choreographers no less than viewers need to support their interpretations by pointing to the visible features of the work.

Intention Versus Meaning

Even as they discuss dances with their makers, student viewers need to avoid equating the original impulses that may have prompted artistic creativity with the "meaning" of a completed work of art. As a work of art develops, it often takes on characteristics that may not have been part of the artist's "original intention." However, the fact that a creative work evolves does not, by itself, guarantee artistic success. Instead it guarantees only that to compose is inherently to discover and to revise, making decisions along the way. Thus, in evaluating any dance, it is important to see clearly what the work *is* and to learn how others see it. The work should not be viewed only in comparison with what the artist might have thought or hoped it would be. An artist's so-called intentions are best regarded as points of departure, not as rules that govern each creative decision or that ensure that the work will be interpreted in only one way—the artist's.

External and Internal Information

One final distinction is relevant to the question of how artists' intentions relate to viewers' critical responses to a work. This is the distinction between the *external facts* about and the *internal features* of a work of art. External facts about a work are such things as possible goals of the artist, details of the artist's personal life, or any nonartistic purposes (e.g., commercial or religious) that might be served by the work. Internal features, on the other hand, are the visible properties of the work itself as these are experienced by the viewers. In a dance, internal features are such things as movements or gestures, the ways these are staged in relation to each other, and the spatial and temporal design of the dance.

Inquiry into the external facts about a work does not reveal the meaning or aesthetic value of a work's internal features. In fact, investigation of external information about a work tends to become so interesting to those who engage in it that critical evaluation of the work's internal features may be entirely forgotten. Such investigations often lose all relevance to the analysis and judgment of the internal features of the work.

This consideration of the relevance of artists' intentions to critical evaluation illustrates a third principle for conducting critical evaluation in the choreography class:

Teaching/Learning Principle

The significance of information about an artist's intention or any external evidence about a work lies solely in the capacity of such information to enhance one's perception of the internal features of that work.

Summary: Important Points to Remember

1. The concept of "intention" may refer either to the goal an artist has in mind in creating a work or to the meanings an artist might hope to express through the completed work.

2. Whatever choreographers might say about their work, it is not safe to assume that a work's true meaning is only what the choreographer says it is.

3. It is also a mistake to assume that dances do, or should, communicate in the linguistic sense. The concept of perceptual communication more adequately describes how a dance may express meanings and ideas.

4. While choreographers' interpretations of their dances should not be given priority, it may be useful for students to hear from a choreographer what principles of art or compositional strategies were used in crafting a dance. This can help students understand how art practice is informed by theory and how various concepts might figure into the choreographic process.

Chapter 5

TEACHER MYTHS ABOUT CRITICAL EVALUATION

This chapter will help you understand

- four common assumptions, or myths, about the students' and teachers' roles in the choreography class. These myths are:
  1. It is the teacher's job to tell students what is "good."
  2. Hearing criticism hurts students' feelings.
  3. Dancers should do dancing, not discuss it.
  4. Students learn to critique dances by making dances.

Because they were once students of dance who themselves received little or no training in critical evaluation, many choreography teachers bring to the classroom the same set of assumptions about viewing art that their students possess.

Many choreography teachers labor under four widely held assumptions, or myths, about the roles students and teachers ought to play in the evaluative process. Analysis of these myths reveals how they tend to lock teachers and their students into a noncritical relationship to works of art, and brings up two more teaching/learning principles upon which the ORDER approach is based.

Myth #1: "It's the Teacher's Job to Tell Students What's Good."

Traditional approaches to teaching choreography (and, indeed, most other subjects) situate the teacher as the critical authority in the classroom. This traditional hierarchy is based on four standard assumptions:

1. Choreography students have only limited dance-viewing experience.
2. Students' knowledge of dance conventions and traditions is scant.
3. Students' artistic taste tends to reflect oversimplified conceptions of art and dance.
4. Students lack the analytical skills necessary to formulate substantive interpretations and critical judgments.

Taken together, these assumptions underlie the notion that while students can personally react to a dance, they cannot truly function in a critical capacity. It follows, then, that the teacher must serve as the critical authority in the class. Placing the teacher in this role is seen as ensuring that student choreographers receive an acceptable level of critical response to their work. It also supposedly causes viewers to learn through imitating their teachers how to carry out "good" critical evaluation.

The key problem with giving a teacher sole critical authority, long recognized by philosophers of art, is that the personal artistic taste and basic critical assumptions of any viewer, even the most sophisticated, affect the viewer's descriptions, analyses, interpretations, and judgments. For this reason, the critical standards and assumptions of all viewers of a work of art need continually to be clarified and examined through class discussion. Until one knows what viewers' critical assumptions are, it is impossible to know what they mean when they express their judgments of a dance. And this applies in particular to the critical responses of teachers in front of a class. In a learning environment where the teacher's critical assumptions are allowed to remain unexplored—but where student dances are rated by the teacher—the students are inevitably left to supplement or eventually replace their unexamined critical assumptions with those conveyed by the teacher.

Granted, the teacher's judgment about a particular dance may well be the best informed and most clearly articulated judgment available to the class. And much of the time, students may agree with their teacher's point of view. But it does not necessarily follow that a teacher's judgment, or anyone else's, is "correct" or that no broader critical discussion is warranted. In fact, to hear or accept only a teacher's judgments in a classroom situation undeservedly elevates those judgments to the status of true propositions and ignores the educational value of critical dialogue.

For a teacher to take the role of sole critical voice, then, in no way guarantees the quality or sufficiency of the critical feedback that student choreographers receive, regardless of the teacher's greater experience as choreographer or as critic. Furthermore, patterning after their teacher does not ensure that student viewers will learn to formulate their own substantive critical responses. Indeed, when a teacher's critical voice dominates in the classroom, students are usually exposed to judgments derived from undiscussed and possibly arbitrary criteria. This diminishes their experience of observing a dance, reflecting on its character, and debating its merits and drawbacks. It also makes instruction more closely resemble indoctrination.

The distinction between *instruction* and *indoctrination* is important for teachers in all disciplines. Indoctrination leads students to adopt the teacher's position or belief without investigating its reasons or evidence. Instruction, on the other hand, includes discussion of the reasons and principles underlying the conclusions being presented. True instruction in how to develop a critical response, therefore, requires systematic inquiry into the standards and assumptions against which each work is being judged and into the relevance of these standards to the work. The distinction between instruction and indoctrination is fundamental to the method for conducting critical evaluation outlined in the next chapter.

The fourth principle for conducting critical evaluation in the choreography class follows:

Teaching/Learning Principle

To foster critical reflection and aesthetic debate among students and to avoid reducing critical evaluation to a process of indoctrination, the teacher's voice should not be the only or the decisive critical voice in a class. It is important that each student be a fully participating member of the critical community formed by the class.

Myth #2: "Hearing Criticism Hurts Students' Feelings."

Many teachers do conduct critical evaluation by holding student discussions in class. But dance educators are usually very sensitive to the moods of their students. This is not surprising, since dancing is an art that often deals with subtle nuances of human expression. As a result of their high degree of sensitivity, however, many dance educators worry that they must protect student choreographers from criticism that is negative or destructive. Underlying this concern are two assumptions:

1. In order to exercise their creative powers fully, students need to feel psychologically safe and secure.
2. Criticism in the form of peer evaluation threatens this kind of security.

All conscientious teachers would agree that student artists should never be subjected to harshly expressed responses consisting entirely of a list of the faults in a particular work. There is no doubt that insensitive delivery of aesthetic judgments can impede a recipient's development as a choreographer. But these are common-sense arguments against doing critical evaluation badly, not reasons to avoid doing it at all.

Doing critical evaluation well involves recognizing, first of all, the significant difference between delivering verbal abuse and offering a thoughtful evaluative response, which may include descriptive interpretations and appraisals or even recommended revisions for the dance. In short, it is important for all involved to remember that the meaning of the term "criticism" also encompasses the concepts of "appreciation" and "praise." There is no reason that critical discussions cannot both address substantive issues and be respectful of the artist.

Sometimes, in their concern for the psychological well-being of student artists, teachers self-consciously censor their own critical responses and may restrict class discussions to brief comments expressing enjoyment of the works presented in class. In these classes, critical evaluation is not truly taking place at all. Moreover, these students will receive little stimulation to define and clarify their own artistic values. For this reason, the following is the fifth teaching/learning principle upon which the ORDER approach is based:

Teaching/Learning Principle

Each participant in a critical discussion should be taught that offering criticism includes expressing appreciation and praise. Students should be encouraged to identify and describe both successful and problematic aspects of the dance under review and to give the choreographer suggestions for possible revisions to the dance.

Myth #3: "Dancers Should Do Dancing, Not Discuss It."

Another traditional attitude that often discourages choreography teachers from practicing critical evaluation in the classroom is the stereotype of the "inarticulate dancer," whose grace and skill in the art of movement are supposedly matched only by her or his lack of interest or ability in intellectual pursuits.

An outgrowth of the belief in the inarticulate dancer is the notion that students' critical abilities develop automatically through the practice of creating dances in class.

The conviction that critical evaluation is uninteresting to or beyond the capacities of dance students has been voiced by many educators. Doris Humphrey (1959), for example, contributes to this view when she asserts not only that the dancer is "notoriously unintellectual," but also that he or she "finds analysis painful and boring" (p. 17). Humphrey also writes that the dancer is "a notoriously nonverbal thinker, and inarticulate as well" (p. 21).

It is highly doubtful that such characterizations of dancers accurately describe contemporary college students of choreography. In any case, many teachers, having lived with this assumption, are tempted to conclude that dance students simply cannot give or receive substantive critical evaluation. These teachers see evaluation as a separate intellectual pursuit more properly handled somewhere outside the dance curriculum.

Certainly critical description, analysis, interpretation, and judgment, as well as the careful observation and reflection from which these arise, do have a philosophical component and require intellectual effort. Moreover, critical discussions among students untrained in critical evaluation may sometimes get bogged down by confusion, misunderstanding, and, occasionally, even bruised egos. But to conclude on that basis that critical evaluation is inappropriate for the choreography class is to confuse two different classroom situations as if they represented a single insurmountable problem. Students may lack the disposition, or willingness, to apply themselves intellectually; or students' capacity, or skills, in the area of philosophical or intellectual pursuits may be undeveloped.

All teachers are surely familiar with these two types of students. The first may only rarely join in discussions of the meanings and merits of the dances seen in class. When they do participate, they may give the impression that they mistrust or are impatient with the critical process. They may seem to have little motivation to improve their own critical skills.

Students of the second type, on the other hand, might join eagerly into critical discussions. But they may nevertheless have difficulty following and assessing the critical arguments of others, testing the merits of rival interpretations and judgments, or making interpretations and judgments of their own.

Unfortunately, teachers often overlook the fact that the same students who exhibit indifference toward critical evaluation might well have the capacity for advanced intellectual endeavors. But these students may never have been shown how stimulating such critical evaluation can be to creativity in dance or how to go about evaluating a dance. Similarly, students who appear to be intellectually unprepared to formulate and assess critical arguments may nonetheless be willing to develop and improve these skills. There is every reason to believe that both types of students can improve with instruction.

Today's dance students, once they have been properly introduced to the practice of critical discourse, are quite capable of engaging in substantive critical evaluation. To view dancers as unintellectual is to lose sight of the fact that critical analysis stimulates students' artistic development.

Myth #4: "Students Learn to Critique Dances by Making Dances."

As mentioned earlier, the tendency to downplay the training of choreography students in critical evaluation is connected with the notion that by creating dances one learns how to assess them. This assumption holds that, through exploring concepts and elements of dance and by making creative choices about movement and structure in the dance, students will automatically develop all the knowledge and skills they need to observe dances with insight. They will learn to formulate sound critical analyses, interpretations, and aesthetic judgments. Critical abilities and understanding are thought to follow creative activity as a sort of intellectual by-product.

Indeed, students' ability to perceive dances clearly and evaluate them carefully may improve somewhat over time with no training. However, some of the flawed critical practices we have reviewed are likely to become ingrained if students receive no formal instruction in the stages of authentic critical evaluation. These flawed approaches include over-reliance on the subjective response, resorting to the use of preset criteria for judgment, and searching for the artist's intentions each time one views a dance.

Another way of looking at this issue is to ask this question: If teachers are expecting students' critical skills to improve through practice, how will students acquire the proper skills in the first place?

Self-Evaluation Is Only Part of Critical Evaluation

Those who suggest that critical skills develop automatically may be erroneously equating self-evaluation—a student's deepening personal knowledge of his or her artistic tendencies, stylistic preferences, and compositional strengths and weaknesses—with critical evaluation in general. But the personal insights drawn from one's own dance-making experiences, while very meaningful, form only one dimension of the perspective needed for substantive critical evaluation. In fact, the stimulation provided by peer criticism has long been recognized as essential to meaningful self-evaluation. As critical theorist George Boas (1937) writes:

> *Self-criticism arises out of the criticism of others; one's own desires are standards until someone questions them. They are standards not only for ourselves but for everyone else. For one naturally believes others to be like us until their difference is proved. When proved it is first not evidence of diversity, but of abnormality. It requires a certain education to be willing to admit that human nature is not all of a piece and that one's own nature is not a fair sample of humanity. (pp. 141-142)*

In other words, the skill of self-evaluation is both developed and improved by training and experience in evaluating the works of others. Unless they have the opportunity to consider and debate the critical remarks of others with respect to a work—that is, to participate in a critical community—people tend to regard their personal artistic assumptions as the standard. Instruction in the theory and practice of critical evaluation, then, helps students to make their critiques constructive and valuable for both their peers and themselves.

The Student Critic's Task

Whenever choreography students assemble to observe and discuss the performance of a dance created by one of their peers, they are, whether they know it or not, functioning as critics rather than audience members. Indeed, students must play the role of critic far more often than they present their own dances to the class. The student critic's task—to formulate a substantive critical response—is not an instantaneous act, however. Rather, it is the result of a systematic process of inquiry into the visible features of the work under review as they have affected the viewers.

Summary: Important Points to Remember

1. The critical standards and assumptions of all viewers need continually to be clarified and examined through class discussion. Until one knows what viewers' critical assumptions are, it is impossible to know what they mean when they express their judgments of a dance.

2. Criticism does not simply mean to find fault with something. The term also encompasses the concepts of appreciation and praise. There is no reason why critical discussions cannot be both substantive and respectful of the artist.

3. It is not enough just to do dancing. Dance students need to learn how to discuss dances as well.

4. Critical skills do not develop automatically as a result of practice in making dances. Choreography students need training and practice in formulating critical responses to the dances seen in class.

PART II

The ORDER Approach to Critical Evaluation

The next five chapters present the ORDER approach to critical evaluation. The ORDER approach divides the critical process into the following five stages, or critical activities:

Observation
Reflection
Discussion
Evaluation
Recommendations for Revisions

In describing the role of each of these activities in the critical process, I blend practical suggestions for doing critical evaluation with explanations of the theoretical considerations underlying each suggestion. This interweaving of theory and practice will foster greater understanding in choreography teachers and students of how the critical process works and why it works as it does.

The five Teaching/Learning Principles upon which the ORDER approach is based are:

1. Subjective, or feeling-based, responses play only a preliminary role in the critical response, and they must not be considered a sufficient basis for making aesthetic judgments because they describe the viewer rather than the dance under review.

2. Critical judgments of a dance should not to be based on predetermined criteria for artistic excellence. Instead, they should be guided by the visible features of the dance and the experience viewers have of those features and their relationships to each other.

3. The significance of information about an artist's intentions or any external evidence about a work lies solely in the capacity of such information to enhance one's perception of the internal features of that work.

4. To foster critical reflection and aesthetic debate among students and to avoid reducing critical evaluation to a process of indoctrination, the teacher's voice should not be the only or the decisive critical voice in a class. It is important that each student be a fully participating member of the critical community formed by the class.

5. Each participant in a critical discussion should be taught that offering criticism includes expressing appreciation and praise. Students should be encouraged to identify and describe both successful and problematic aspects of the dance under review and to give the choreographer suggestions for possible revisions to the dance.

Chapter 6

OBSERVATION

This chapter will help you understand

- the difference between casually looking at and carefully observing a work of art,
- the importance of perceptual openness on the part of the viewer in watching a dance, and
- the importance of noticing during observation.

In contrast to the relatively unfocused and incomplete perceptual attention one usually devotes to the objects and events in one's immediate surroundings, observation of a work of art requires a different kind of mental alertness. Attention needs to be deliberately concentrated upon the work of art, consciously isolating it, in order to perceive it as it presents itself. During observation of a dance, therefore, it is essential for the viewer to focus on being open and receptive to the experience.

Perceptual Openness

Perceptual openness is a matter of active control: Critical viewers must make a point of opening their minds to an experience. It is not sufficient to sit back and allow the experience to be filtered and distorted through unexamined beliefs, critical assumptions, or emotions. To encourage openness in student observers of a dance, teachers should remind the class often of the importance of mentally putting aside, before watching a dance, any suppositions or expectations that might prejudice observation of the work and subsequent critical evaluation. In other words, viewers must do for themselves what a frame does for a picture: tighten the focus of their concentration from the total field of vision to that portion of the field occupied by the work of art. In observing a dance, this means focusing on the space, both literal and figurative, in which the dance takes place. But a dance not only occupies space, it unfolds over time as well. Thus, observing a dance well means focusing on the work for the duration of its performance.

To ensure that viewers' total attention is directed toward the performance in a classroom situation, the performers should not begin until all the viewers are settled and ready to attend to the dance. In addition, at the end of the performance, dancers should hold their final positions for a moment so that it is clear when the dance is over.

Viewers' Role:

1. Attend to the dance with an open mind for the duration of its performance.

2. Tighten perceptual focus to include only the dance itself.

3. Set aside artistic assumptions, preferences, expectations.

Performers' Role:

1. Do not begin until all viewers are quiet and focused.

2. Hold final position for a moment to make the ending clear.

Noticing Versus Recognizing

To become sharp observers, students need to focus on *noticing* as much as they can about each dance observed, instead of merely looking for familiar or predetermined choreographic elements. There is a crucial difference between recognizing and noticing, as art educator David Perkins (1981, 78-79) has pointed out. Perkins explains that in *recognizing*, observers try to find familiar aspects in whatever they are looking at. For example, while watching a dance, viewers might look for graceful movements, pointed feet, and high jumps. But viewing a dance with such preconceived notions in mind restricts from the outset what may be seen in the dance by stipulating before it begins what kinds of elements are to be recognized. Other aspects of the work are likely to pass by unseen.

The viewer who concentrates on recognizing and classifying components of a dance during observation tends to experience the work only as a series of individual moments, each flickering briefly in consciousness but unrelated to the work as a whole. Noticing, on the other hand, is a kind of attentiveness in which observers do not look specifically for certain things, but remain open to aspects of the work that may otherwise be overlooked. Encouraging students to allow themselves to notice whatever they can about a dance lets them see it as an aesthetic whole rather than as a conglomeration of elements, some of which have been designated as "important" to look for.

Sample Observation Exercise

A very simple in-class exercise can help students become conscious of how they observe and make them aware of pitfalls in the observation process. Divide the students into pairs and ask one student in each pair to speak his or her thoughts aloud to the other in a stream-of-consciousness manner during the performance of a short dance. The student in each pair who is not talking listens carefully to, and makes brief notes of, what the speaker says. After the dance is performed, the note taker shares with the speaker what he or she said while the dance was being performed. Did the speaker remark upon specific aspects of the dance? If so, how general or detailed were the speaker's descriptive observations? What other kinds of remarks did the speaker make? Did the speaker talk about his or her own feelings? Did the speaker make immediate judgments of the dance? Ideally, the speakers will make clear descriptive remarks that indicate they are both willing to and capable of focusing on the dance as it reveals itself through the performance.

The analysis of spontaneous critical statements in this exercise increases students' awareness of how mental constructs such as emotional responses and normative judgments can intrude upon the ostensibly quiet observation of a dance. The insights gained from this exercise and their contribution to the experience of observing each dance without mental distractions are fundamental to the practice of critical evaluation. This kind of focused observation will be key to two later steps in the ORDER approach: reflection on and discussion of the work.

THINK ON IT
Ideas for Writing and Discussion

Have you ever been extremely aware of your surroundings, noticing subtle details in or about your environment? In what kinds of situations has this occurred? Describe your experience, and consider how this kind of conscious awareness is different from ordinary waking consciousness. How can critics train themselves to bring about this heightened state of awareness while watching the performance of a dance?

Summary: Important Points to Remember

1. Evaluation of any work of art begins with and depends upon careful observation. Observation is not in itself a form of criticism but is a mode of awareness that prepares students to describe, analyze, interpret, and evaluate dances.

2. Careful observation of a work of art differs from everyday observation, in which we think about objects and events in terms of their use and importance and tend not to notice their aesthetic qualities.

Chapter 7

REFLECTION

This chapter will help you understand

- how reflective writing following the observation of a dance helps you both to see a dance more clearly and to deliver precise feedback to the choreographer,

- the importance of using clear and precise language in describing and analyzing the dances you see in class,

- how to guard against the influence of unexamined assumptions about art upon your critical responses, and

- the distinction between intrinsic and extrinsic features of art and the role of each in critical evaluation.

Untrained observers usually rush to judge works of art before having reflected on them. One of the goals of artistic training, therefore, should be the development of what art educator Edmund B. Feldman (1971) calls a "judicious temperament." In using this term, Feldman means

> . . . *the ability to withhold judgment until all the evidence is in . . . Persons untrained in art criticism . . . state conclusions first and then set about finding reasons why their conclusions are valid. . . . But the virtue of a judicious temperament is the ability to allow time for the multitude of impressions, associations, sensations, and half-formed judgments to interact, to permit intelligence to operate in the task of sifting, sorting, and organizing. (p. 616)*

In the ORDER approach, a reflection period of several minutes immediately follows the completion of a performance. During reflection, students have an opportunity to clarify and record their impressions of the structures and artistic qualities they perceived in the work before giving the choreographer any verbal response to the dance or formulating interpretations and judgments of the dance. Accordingly, the reflective period may be thought of, adopting the terminology of art educator Ralph Smith (1973), as "exploratory aesthetic criticism" (p. 39). The exploratory phase trains students to notice and describe choreographic patterns; to distinguish differences, similarities, and relationships among artistic qualities; and to perceive the part/whole relationships within the work.

The Goals of Reflective Writing

During critical reflection, viewers spend two to five minutes writing brief notes describing and analyzing the dance under review. Students for whom the dance evoked strong feelings may wish to begin the reflective writing period by mentioning these feelings. However, students should be encouraged to proceed from noting their feelings to describing and analyzing the visible features of the dance—while taking note of emotional reactions can be a meaningful step toward articulating critical opinions, the relevance of one's feelings about a work to criticism can be determined only through a rigorous examination of the connections between those feelings and the visible features of the work.

Whether or not students include accounts of their feeling-based responses to the work in their initial reflective writing, combining critical reflection with putting thoughts on paper helps students develop and explore their understanding of the dance on their own. The writing step bridges the gap between silent and spoken critical appraisal by leading students consciously to consider and reconsider the nature and the effects of properties of the dance before pooling their responses with those of the other viewers. Reflective writing enables students to organize into words the details of their perceptions of the dance so that they can share them with others.

Initiating Focused Freewriting

Reflective writing is a kind of *focused freewriting*, a term adopted from the discipline of expository writing. Focused freewriting is informal writing that helps students become conscious of the nature of their perceptual experience before hearing the responses of others.

Focused freewriting about a particular dance may be initiated by asking students immediately after a dance has been presented,

1. "What did you notice in this dance?"
2. "Did your attention to the dance fluctuate during the performance? When and in what ways?"

Writing in response to these questions is easy for students because there is no pressure to construct a persuasive critical response. Students can concentrate solely on consolidating their own perceptions of the dance into a clear description of what they experienced as its salient features.

Teaching Hints

It is difficult for some students to concentrate during silent reflection or to remember what they have seen. These students tend to finish writing sooner than everyone else and their descriptions tend to be sparse. Encourage these students to write without self-censoring, allowing reflective memory of the work to emerge without worrying about which words to use. Encourage them also to write in greater detail about what they do remember about the dance. These steps will improve their ability to engage in critical reflection.

Describing the Dance

When students begin their focused freewriting after viewing a dance, they should concentrate on description and analysis of the visible properties of the dance. The viewers' only aim in describing the dance is to identify what they saw in the work as fully as possible rather than to formulate interpretations of the work's meaning(s) or judgments of its merit. Reflective description, Feldman (1971) says, is thus a process

> . . . of taking inventory, of noting what is immediately presented to the viewer. We are interested at this stage in avoiding, as far as possible, the drawing of inferences. We wish to arrive at a simple account of "what is there," the kind of account with which any reasonably observant person would agree. (p. 635)

The primary focus for a description of a dance is thus its particular movements, gestures, and shapes, as well as perceived energy qualities and dynamics, structural patterns, sounds, and overall choreographic design characteristics. The following sample descriptions offer contrast:

Vague, general description

Lots of dancers moving at the same time. Big movements. Circular and linear patterns. No musical accompaniment.

Precise, detailed description

Opening section of six dancers in unison; circular leaping pattern with sudden changes of direction. All three levels used. Changes in tempo create in-and-out-of-unison effect. Dancers' breath and footfalls create rhythmic sound score. Circular pattern gives way to two diagonal lines of three dancers.

In formulating detailed reflective descriptions, viewers must strive to recall often subtle features of the dance such as its overall structural properties and its use of focus, energy, and gesture. But while reflection involves the mental restructuring of perceptual experience, reflective writing is neither an interpretive nor a creative process. The viewers' aim is to achieve a greater awareness of the sensuous features of the dance, not to invent stories about the work or articulate impressions about its meaning.

The Language of Description

In describing a dance, viewers should try to utilize *low-inference*, or *unloaded*, language. The following sample passages describing the beginning of a dance illustrate the difference between low- and high-inference descriptive language:

High-inference *(loaded language)*

The four dancers moved in a totally predictable pattern from the outside to the center of their world. The leader of this group moved with powerful, domineering movements while the followers seemed frightened and timid.

Low-inference *(unloaded language)*

The four dancers moved toward the center, one from each of the four corners of the stage. Three of the dancers moved with small steps and appeared to be lightly floating, while the fourth moved with larger, heavier movements and stronger energy.

The first sample contains interpretive and judgmental terms and inferences, showing that the writer did not formulate a precise (or open-minded) view of the aesthetic aspects of the dance. Instead, this writer made an interpretive assumption that each dancer represented a character in a drama and also delivered a judgment of the choreographic design ("a totally predictable pattern"). It is possible that in further analysis of the dance, the writer may eventually supply evidence to support these remarks. But for this writer, the critical reflection period has failed to promote articulation of the basic perceptions necessary to support interpretive and evaluative claims.

THINK ON IT
Ideas for Writing and Discussion

Reflect again on the distinction between loaded and unloaded language as you consider the two contexts below:

1. Newspaper editorials
2. Political speeches

How does loaded language operate in each of these contexts? In what ways do journalists and political candidates use loaded language? Do such uses of loaded language tend to inform us or mislead us?

The Danger of Critical Assumptions

Many times, viewers whose initial reflective accounts are loaded with interpretive speculations and veiled judgments are looking at the work, perhaps unknowingly, through the narrow perspective of a particular critical assumption. There are five common critical assumptions that often interfere with critics' perception and appreciation of art.

The realist assumption holds that the excellence of a work of art is dependent upon the accuracy with which it depicts, copies, or symbolizes something from nature, myth, or literature. Viewers who hold this assumption expect dances always to tell stories or to depict dramatic characters interacting with one another. This assumption often leads students to classify dances in which there are no dramatic situations, such as non-narrative or abstract dances, as poor works.

The formal assumption holds that the excellence of a work of art is dependent upon the perfection of its form and structure. This criterion is objective in the sense that the perception of form and structure is not dependent upon the arbitrary emotional responses of each viewer. But it overlooks the possibility that structural perfection, if there is such a thing, may make one work exciting while making another work bland. The excellence of some works may lie in their chaotic or oddly proportioned structure.

The expressionist assumption holds that the excellence of a work of art is dependent upon how accurately it transmits to the observer an experience or idea that was born in the mind of the artist. This assumption leads many students to view works of art simply as vehicles of linguistic communication between an artist and a spectator. However, as dance educators Milton Snoeyenbos and Carole Knapp (1979) point out, many dances focus "on movement itself, and not on movement as a medium for the conveyance of emotions, attitudes or opinions. . . ." (p. 20)

The emotional assumption holds that the excellence of a work of art is dependent upon the intensity of the emotion it arouses in an observer. This assumption leads many students to concern themselves not with the visible properties of the work in question, but rather with their own emotional reaction to the work.

The originality assumption holds that the excellence of a work of art is dependent upon its novelty, shock value, trendiness, or the freshness of its approach. This assumption leads many viewers to simply compare the work under review with other works rather than fully analyze its aesthetic properties.

It is important that choreography teachers introduce and discuss these assumptions with their students, pointing out that astute observers must consciously work on reducing the influence of any blanket assumptions, which can distort one's perceptions of works of art.

Analyzing Relationships

Reflective analysis is, in Feldman's (1971) words, a type of extended description in which the viewer describes "the relations among qualities . . . which are responsible for the existence of the things and subjects included in our descriptive inventory" (p. 637). In the reflective analysis stage, then, viewers move from the identification of the visible properties of the work to writing about the way they think these properties interacted with one another in the work.

For example, one dancer may obscure our perception of another; one group may echo or perhaps foreshadow the movements of another group; one section of the dance may consist of movements that speed up, slow down, or in some other way relate to (or contrast with) the movements of another section. Accounts of the formal relationships between and among the dancers and the parts of the dance are appropriate concerns of the critic during the analysis stage of critical reflection.

Like reflective description, analysis is concerned only with what the viewer perceived in the dance rather than with the formulation of interpretive explanations of the subject matter or meaning of the dance. This is an important point, for it is in making the move from description to analysis that untrained viewers often drift away from the visible properties of the work and jump ahead to the interpretation of it. However, interpretations need to be supported by the evidence and the insights gained through description and analysis.

Intrinsic and Extrinsic Features of Art

Reflective description and analysis of a dance, then, involve concentrating exclusively on identifying and characterizing the relations among the work's *intrinsic* (visible) features and deferring interpretations and judgments of the work, setting aside all knowledge and speculation about such *extrinsic* elements as the presumed intentions of the choreographer or other facts about the origins of the work. Anything not directly perceivable during observation is not relevant to the description and analysis stages. Reflection is not for "figuring out" the dance—i.e., translating, paraphrasing, or interpreting it. Rather, it is a time for recording in words one's perceptions of the dance as it was experienced during observation.

Types of Formal Relationships

Janet Adshead et al. (1988, p. 119) identify five kinds of formal relationships within dances that students might describe in their reflective notes:

1. relations within a single movement or between movements;
2. simple or complex relations of elements occurring at a point in time;
3. relations through time such as repetitions and variations;
4. relations between any single moment and the linear development of the dance; and
5. major and minor subsidiary relations among phrases and sections of the dance.

Teachers in beginning-level courses can help students learn to identify these relationships by pointing them out during observation of one or more short dances seen during the class period. In addition, familiarizing students with the basic descriptive vocabulary for movement developed by Rudolf Laban (1971) can also help them learn to describe and analyze dances. Laban's system, at its most basic level, provides pairs of opposite terms that help students perceive a dancer's use of *weight, space, time,* and *flow.*

WEIGHT can be seen as strong or light

SPACE can be seen as near to the body or far from the body

TIME can be seen as quick or sustained

FLOW can be seen as free or bound

Familiarity with these basic concepts helps students to notice subtle aspects of the dance under review and to describe and analyze it clearly.

The Importance of Reflection

Unlike critical approaches in which an immediate oral response is expected from students, the ORDER approach ensures that discussion of a work is dominated neither by the most eloquent students nor by those quickest to offer interpretations or judgments. It does this by devoting the first several minutes after each dance has been observed to reflective description and analysis of the work through focused freewriting. As a pedagogical tool for enhancing students' ability to define their own perceptions, reflective critical writing is a valuable supplement to spoken discourse. The writing process allows students to generate a tangible record of the evolution of their reflective insights. Reflective writing therefore enables teachers systematically to introduce and explore with students the distinctions between such concepts as

1. noticing and recognizing,
2. intrinsic and extrinsic features of art, and
3. individual (private) and shared (public) perceptual experience.

While each of these pairs may be investigated through discussion alone, such inquiry is greatly facilitated when students share reflective notes. These notes crystallize specific observations and the precise language used to express them, which might otherwise be overlooked during the course of a discussion. Moreover, writing reflectively about the dance under review before moving to discussion discourages rushing from viewing to interpreting and evaluating the work. Students can see how aesthetic appraisals often change during the initial contemplative period as first impressions are modified through reflection.

THINK ON IT
Ideas for Writing and Discussion

We have been considering how a person's ability to discuss a work of art is enhanced by first taking a few minutes to reflect upon his or her experience of the work. But is the reflective process useful only in aesthetic contexts? What other situations can you think of in which it would be helpful to stop and think, and maybe even write down some thoughts, before speaking or taking action?

The Choreographer's Role During Reflection

During the reflective writing stage, the choreographer whose dance has just been seen should also be writing—about the experience of having created and presented the dance. Reflective writing by choreographers allows them to reconsider their process of conceiving and developing the dance, how they expected the viewers to react, and what parts of the dance they think still present questions or problems. Choreographers may also wish to reflect upon the thoughts and feelings they experienced while performing the dance or watching its performance. Reflective writing gives student choreographers an opportunity both to anticipate and to observe their own learning process, enabling them to become more autonomous learners who are less reliant on the information and authority of others. Moreover, critical reflection on the concluded performances of their dances can lead choreographers to understand which aspects of their works have been seen in a similar light by viewers.

Even though the experiences of creating and performing a dance may be, at least in part, nonlinguistic, they are not irrational, nor is reflective writing about such experiences futile. It is worthwhile for choreographers to engage in reflective writing as a prelude to discussion not because nonlinguistic experiences such as dance are flawed or incomplete, but because verbalizing thoughts about such experiences helps to better understand them. Taken as a whole, then, the writing component of this second stage of critical evaluation paves the way for focused discussion of the dance under review, which is the primary goal of having students share their work with the class.

Summary: Important Points to Remember

1. The reflection period of exploratory description and analysis following the observation of a dance trains students to describe a work's choreographic patterns; to distinguish differences, similarities, and relationships among artistic qualities; and to perceive the part/whole relationships in the work.

2. Exploratory writing bridges the gap between silent and spoken critical appraisal by leading students consciously to consider and reconsider the nature and the effects of properties of the dance before pooling their responses with those of the other viewers.

3. Good critics will consciously work on reducing the influence of any blanket assumptions, which can distort one's perceptions of works of art.

4. The reflective stage of critical evaluation involves concentrating on describing and analyzing the intrinsic features of a work while setting aside all knowledge and speculation about such extrinsic elements as the motives of the choreographer or other facts about the origins of the work.

5. Reflective writing gives student choreographers an opportunity both to anticipate and to observe their own learning process, enabling them to become more autonomous learners who are less reliant on the information and authority of others.

Chapter 8

DISCUSSION

This chapter will help you understand

- the first stages of a critical discussion: description and analysis, and interpretation,
- the ways discussion can improve viewers' perception and appreciation of dances and help choreographers as they continue to develop their dances, and
- how reflective description and analysis help one to formulate clear and defensible interpretations and judgments of works of art.

The reflective stage of critical evaluation is followed by a discussion based on the students' descriptive and analytical notes. Group discussions tend to be most successful when the participants direct their remarks to one another rather than to a leader or teacher. Thus, during the discussion it is a good idea for the students to sit in a circle or semicircle so they can directly address one another.

Taking turns is important during the initial stage of discussion, when each participant summarizes his or her descriptions of the dance. Taking turns allows each participant to be heard and prevents any one student's monopolizing the discussion. After the discussion gets under way, strict turn-taking is no longer necessary. The discussion may adopt a fairly fluid form, with each speaker recognizing and calling upon the next speaker.

The teacher's role during discussion is to act as facilitator for the group, steering the discussion if it appears to be stalling or turning into a debate between two or three particularly vocal students. The choreographer whose dance is under review simply listens to the discussion as reflective notes are shared.

Teaching Hints

Don't worry if there are periods of silence during discussion. As students learn to listen to one another, they become more reflective and tend to think carefully before speaking. If you sense genuine confusion or hesitancy to proceed among the students, use simple clarifying questions such as "What do you mean?"; "Could you say that another way?"; or "What do the rest of you think about that?" to get discussion moving again.

The Importance of Sharing Reflective Notes

Having all the students share their notes with the group allows them to discover which of their experiences of the dance have also been experienced by others—that is, which aspects may be seen as "public" (as opposed to "private") experiences. The initial stage of the discussion, therefore, demonstrates that, while all viewers may have been presented with the same dance, not everyone has had the same perceptual experience of it. In other words, no description or analysis of a work of art is ever all-encompassing.

The initial stage of the critical discussion helps students see that their preliminary reflective understandings of the dance are related to, but distinct from, their subsequent interpretations and judgments of the work. Basic understanding guides the activities of interpretation and judgment. Conversely, interpretations and judgments enlarge, validate, and even correct understanding.

In the choreography class, then, reflective notes provide the foundation for interpretive and evaluative discussion by supplying the group with some shared background of understanding. By sharing what they have noticed about the dance under review, the students prepare themselves to interpret and judge the work in the later stages of discussion with maximum clarity.

Discussion Stage 1: Description and Analysis

The first stage of discussion in the critical evaluation process, sharing reflective description and analysis, requires more from the students than merely listening to each other's reflective accounts. It also requires participants to seek clarification of others' reflections and to draw attention to details of the dance that may have been overlooked. The give-and-take of this stage of critical discussion allows viewers to extend the scope of their reflective attention in two ways: They become aware of more properties of the dance than they initially noticed, and, with encouragement, they consider more carefully the significance of the properties they did notice. In opening up to viewers new and unexpected perspectives on their experiences of the dance, this discussion can be very helpful to those whose descriptions are unclear or lack detail.

Discussion Stage 2: Interpretation

After reflective notes have been shared and their details clarified, students are invited to volunteer interpretations of the work. If students have perceived visible features of the work as expressing particular ideas, the interpretive stage of the discussion is for the articulation and debate of these.

What Is Interpretation?

While there is scant agreement among philosophers of art on how to achieve a valid interpretation, there is general consensus on two points: One is that interpretation is a process through which the critic articulates his or her view of the meaning(s) of the work, and the other is that plausible interpretations are grounded in description and analysis of the work. As Feldman (1971) puts it, interpretation "directs attention to the import of what we have described and analyzed" (p. 646).

Correspondingly, there are two important points about interpretation for teachers to make clear to student viewers. These points are best stated as negative propositions:

1. The interpretation phase is *not* an invitation to create a story about the work. To interpret a work is not a random or free-associative process, nor is it focused upon the emotions the work may arouse in the viewer.

2. To interpret a work of art is *not* to drift into psychological speculations about the artist who created the work. This is a propensity that may be recognized by the occurrence of remarks ostensibly made about the dance, but that actually refer to the possible emotional motivations of the choreographer. If a student invents stories about the work or tries to make psychological assertions about the choreographer, it is time for the discussion to be gently steered back toward more relevant terrain—i.e., the visible features of the work identified during reflection.

This does not mean, however, that the sole reason for reflectively describing and analyzing a dance is to pave the way for interpretation and judgment. On the contrary, description and analysis have the capacity to greatly enhance perception and appreciation of a work of art for the critic and for anyone who hears that critic's reflections, whether or not any interpretive or evaluative claims follow.

The interpretative stage of the critical discussion is both a continuation of the process of reflectively describing the work under review and a separate stage of criticism during which the viewers move toward making sense of the work. In formulating interpretive hypotheses about a dance's meaning and accepting or rejecting alternative interpretations, the viewers must continually make specific reference to the visible properties of the work.

To interpret a work of art—i.e., to move from describing it to making claims about its meaning(s)—requires a critic to give reasons why others should see the work as he or she sees it. Thus, the claims made during interpretive discussion (and later during the evaluative stage of the discussion) are subject to challenge. The interpretive stage of the discussion is, therefore, again adopting the terminology of Ralph Smith (1973), a mode of "argumentative criticism" (p. 39). It is during this stage that each participant may attempt, as Smith puts it, "to persuade others that the object is in fact reasonably seen, heard, or taken" in the way her or his interpretation or judgment has stated (p. 44).

Accordingly, during this stage of the discussion, participants continue to listen carefully to the remarks of others. The aim of the participants is twofold: to check the *referential adequacy* (i.e., the descriptive accuracy) of any interpretive claims, and to discover and assess the reasons underlying each viewer's claims about meaning in the work.

It is important to note that while interpretations of the dance may well have been implied in reflective notes and partially articulated during the initial stage of the discussion, their full development and articulation properly occurs during the interpretive stage—*after* reflective descriptions and analyses have been discussed.

Interpretive Pluralism

The character and tone of interpretive discussion will no doubt differ from dance to dance. Some dances will generate little discussion because their meaning is immediately understood by the group. Other works may spark vigorous interpretive debate.

It is not uncommon for a dance to generate more than one plausible interpretation or for viewers to formulate different reasons for the same interpretation. Still other works might hint that they express something in particular, but it may be difficult for anyone to adequately describe or demonstrate what it is.

Different critics often interpret dances (and other works of art) in varied ways. This occurs because properties of a work—phrasing or spatial patterns, for example—might receive more or less emphasis in different critics' interpretations. And even when two critics emphasize the same features of a work in their respective interpretations, the meaning each critic finds in those features may differ greatly. Such cases call attention to the importance of the persuasive, or argumentative, nature of interpretive discourse. Critics must make as strong a case as possible to others that the work should be understood their way. Sometimes more than one interpretation will be plausible—that is, supported by the visible properties of the work. This does not mean that there has been an error in interpretation or that the work under review is a poor one. It means simply that the work is *ambiguous*, or capable of supporting multiple interpretations.

It is important to distinguish artistic *ambiguity* from artistic *vagueness*. The former term describes a work that is capable of supporting more than one interpretation, and the latter describes a work that is unable to support any interpretation. Vagueness is something to be avoided in art-making, but ambiguity is something to be valued.

Artists' Contributions to Interpretive Discussion

It is appropriate for the choreographer of the work under review to join in the discussion at this point to seek clarification of any interpretive remarks made by others or to volunteer his or her own interpretations of the dance. However, during the argumentative stage of the discussion, a choreographer whose dance is under review must try to maintain an open-minded attitude toward the interpretive remarks volunteered by the viewers. The choreographer, and indeed all the participants, must seek to fully understand the others' interpretations before challenging them. This means that initial responses to others' remarks should take the form of questions to elicit greater detail and clarity. After interpretive remarks have been made clear—i.e., when their precise meanings and supporting evidence have been established—it is appropriate for participants to challenge their content.

It can be interesting during the interpretive discussion phase to discuss an artist's interpretations of or intentions in the work under review. However, it is important to remember that artists' accounts of the meaning of their works should never be valued over those advanced by other viewers. An artist's statements, like those of the other

Teaching Hints

As students learn to articulate their own critical responses and to explore those of their peers, they occasionally experience difficulty both in questioning or challenging each other and in answering the questions and challenges posed to them by others. If discussion appears to be stalling while students debate interpretive claims, use clarifying remarks and questions such as "I think what Juana means is . . . .Is that right, Juana?" and "Can you state that another way, James? It is not quite clear what you mean" to move the discussion along. Remind students often that the aim of this stage of the discussion is not to "win" the argument. It is, rather, the mutual exploration of the viewers' perceptions of the meaning(s) of the dance under review.

participants, must be supported by the visible properties of the work itself in order to be relevant to the discussion of that work.

General Explanations and Artistic Justifications

When listening to artists' accounts of the origins or meanings of their works, viewers should keep in mind the distinction between a *general explanation* and an *artistic justification* for the artist's having made a particular choice in the work. This distinction is subtle but very important in the context of the choreography class. When viewers ask a choreographer such questions as, "Why does everyone fall to the floor in the middle of the first section?" what the viewers are actually asking for has to do with the artist's handling of the conceptual and aesthetic problems of dance-making, not a general explanation that may or may not relate to the problems of dance-making per se.

Consider the following example: A choreographer, Ann, answers the above question by saying, "Everyone falls to the floor right then because I ran out of time to work on that section." With this reply,

Ann gives an explanation for the dancers' falling to the floor in her dance, but she does not provide any artistic justification for having the dancers fall to the floor. Thus, for students to make further comments based on her explanation will only carry the discussion away from relevant critical discourse. For example, someone might suggest that Ann consider scheduling extra rehearsal time in order to fully develop her movement ideas, an idea Ann has probably already considered. Whether she has or has not considered it, however, the suggestion is not directly relevant to the task at hand, which is to critique Ann's dance.

But suppose Ann says, "The dancers fall to the floor because it was important to me to break the spell of the dance right there, to make time suddenly stand still." This reply differs enormously in character from the first. It is an artistic justification indicating that her concern with a particular aesthetic concept or principle prompted her to direct the dancers to fall to the floor. Moreover, this reply makes possible further critical discussion of, for example, the aesthetic principle Ann had in mind, the manner in which she chose to apply that principle, alternative ways she might have applied it, and the relationship between this principle and others employed elsewhere in the dance.

Three Key Points

In considering artists' statements about their work during an interpretive discussion, it is important to keep the following three points in mind:

1. The aim of critical discussion is not to rank or evaluate whatever artistic rules or principles are evident in the dance, but to assess *how* artistic principles are operating in the work. These principles may correspond to an existing theory of art; they may have recently been formulated by the artist to guide the making of this particular work; they may be many or few in number, rigidly or loosely applied, based on random chance, or mathematically derived. The discussion of how artistic principles operate in the work will ideally be a main focus as students discuss any dance.

2. Choreographers may not always be aware of the correspondence between each aspect of their works and specific artistic principles. It may be that Ann, for example, had no particular artistic motive in mind when she directed the dancers to fall to the floor at the end of the dance. She may only have had an intuition to do so. If

this is the case, the discussion of this section of the dance may well shift to a consideration of the artistic principles or choreographic devices the viewers alone perceive as being at work in that section of the dance.

A discussion along these lines will help Ann to discover the nature of artistic conventions, concepts, and principles that appear to the viewers to be operating in her dance even though she is not claiming to have employed them consciously. Such a discussion also shows the viewers that various aspects of the work with which they associate meaning may not be aspects for which Ann had any predetermined intention.

3. The educational value to all students of making the discoveries just mentioned is that they reinforce the idea that substantive critical evaluation can play a valuable role in the creative process. Moreover, these discoveries help students to see that art-making is a process of revision through which the artist develops the work-in-progress by considering both what it is at any given moment and what it can become through further effort.

It is important for the conducting of a critical discussion, then, that the distinction between general explanations and artistic justifications be understood, so that students do not deliver or respond to the former as if they were the latter. However, this distinction should not be interpreted as stipulating a criterion for artistic success. In other words, a dance is not considered good or poor just because the choreographer has (or doesn't have) an artistic justification for each of the aesthetic principles it exhibits.

Summary: Important Points to Remember

1. Group discussions work best when the participants direct their remarks to one another rather than to a leader or teacher. It is a good idea for the students to sit in a circle or semicircle during a discussion so they can directly address one another.

2. The sharing of reflective descriptions and analyses provides the basis for interpretive discussion.

3. All the participants in a critical discussion must seek to fully understand others' interpretations before challenging them.

Appropriate initial responses to others' remarks take the form of questions designed to elicit greater detail and clarity.

4. Interpretation is both a continuation of the process of reflectively describing the work under review and a separate stage of criticism during which the viewers make sense of the work.

5. While it may be helpful for the viewers to hear the choreographer's intentions, an artist's statements, like those of the other participants, must be supported by the visible properties of the work itself in order to be relevant to the discussion of that work.

Chapter 9

EVALUATION

This chapter will help you understand

- how a judgment is different from a guess, a fact, or a feeling,
- how to support an aesthetic judgment about a work of art,
- how aesthetic judgments differ from comparative judgments, and
- the ladder of aesthetic inquiry: criticism, metacriticism, theory, and metatheory.

The third stage of the critical discussion is evaluation or judgment of the dance. As discussed in chapter 5, some educators avoid evaluation because they believe that it stifles creative experimentation. But they overlook the fact that evaluation is going on all the time in education and, as art educator Elliot W. Eisner (1974) argues, not to evaluate students' art work "is to be educationally irresponsible" (p. 97). Eisner further recognizes that "imposition, interference, and insensitive appraisal" can indeed hamper the development of student artists, but this only argues against a certain kind of evaluative process, not against evaluation generally. Moreover, students value thoughtful criticism because it testifies that others are taking their work seriously (p. 97). The key to evaluating dances in the choreography class, then, is to make sure that the concept of judgment is well understood by students and is undertaken with courtesy toward the artist whose work is under review.

The Concept of Judgment

Because the very concept of judgment often confuses and intimidates students, they need to spend some time discussing the meaning and use of the term. *Judgment*, according to education theorist Thomas F. Green (1971), includes ranking, estimating, predicting, and adjudicating. Green points out that each of these concepts is distinct from the others in certain respects, "but in this one respect—that they involve standards, grounds, or reasons—they are quite alike" (p. 175). It is dependence upon reasonable grounds that elevates judgments beyond mere guesses or hunches, which, as Green characterizes them, are "groundless, or very nearly groundless" (p. 175).

Yet if judging is not a matter of guessing, neither is it a matter of knowing. Green writes:

> *When we are wholly without any grounds for ranking, estimating, or predicting, then we cannot be said to be in a position to render a judgment. But conversely, when our grounds or evidence are conclusive, then we do not need to render a judgment. (p. 176)*

The idea that judgments are not certain but are subject to reconsideration and change in the light of new evidence underscores the importance of detailed description and analysis as fundamental components of critical evaluation. Using Green's terminology again, judgments are both "informative" and "directive." By citing features of the work identified through reflective description and analysis, viewers inform others of their reasons for judging a particular work as good, bad, or average, and in so doing urge others to see it this way.

Judgments Are Not Feelings

Just as judging is not a matter of knowing or guessing, it is also not a matter of feeling. It is important for students to understand this, for the remark "This dance stimulates me—I like it" may mistakenly be construed as an aesthetic judgment when it is not. It is, rather, an expression of an opinion that is entirely subjective. And because such opinions are beyond the reach of reasonable argument, there is no disagreement between Anita and Malcolm when Anita says "It stimulates me—I like it" and Malcolm says "It bores me—I don't like it." Such statements are not judgments because they include no information about the dance. Genuine aesthetic judgments make specific reference to the intrinsic features of the work under review and thus are not the same as subjective preferences.

It is important, therefore, for teachers to point out to students the distinction between personal likings and substantive evaluation. As Green notes, it is incorrect to think of "a prizing or valuation" as a judgment, because "An act of appraisal is an estimate of a thing's value . . . an act of prizing is a bestowal of value on a thing" (p. 183). Accordingly, the viewer who says, "It's stimulating—I like it" is actually expressing a personal valuation that neither directs others' attention to any particular feature of the dance nor justifies the implied link between the viewer's feeling-based response and the aesthetic quality of the dance.

Judgments Are Not Facts

While judgments may adopt the same grammatical form as objective claims, this does not make them statements of fact. For example, while the judgment, "The dance is rather poorly constructed" and the factual assertion, "The dance is six minutes long" are grammatically similar, they are different kinds of statements. Because the duration of the dance can be measured, any statement about its length is not a judgment of the dance, but rather a factual statement about the dance that may be easily verified by timing the dance.

A statement about the excellence (or lack thereof) of the construction of the work, on the other hand, is a judgment. But in making such a judgment, one does not aim to prove an objective fact about the construction of the dance. Rather, one aims through description and analysis to persuade others to review the perceptual evidence— i.e., the work itself—and make the same assessment the viewer has made. Thus, judgments are negotiable in a way that factual claims are not. Factual claims, when true, are binding. If the dance is six minutes long, it is six minutes long for every viewer. Aesthetic judgments, on the other hand, are never binding in this way. The judgment that the dance is "poorly constructed" is always subject to challenge and revision in light of more detailed or insightful description and analysis of the work.

Teaching Hints

Even after the concept of judgment has been explained to them, students often hesitate to articulate evaluations of each other's works. For many students it is difficult to overcome the assumption that judgments are inherently "destructive."

Be patient with these students and do not insist that they evaluate each dance seen in class. Encourage them to re-read and to think about the points discussed in this chapter and to remember that a judgment is simply a description of what one sees as "working" or "not working" in the work under review.

Evaluative Pluralism

Like interpretations, judgments can legitimately differ with respect to a particular work of art. To justify an aesthetic judgment of a dance and make it persuasive, one must clearly describe the precise manner in which the choreographer has structured and manipulated the materials of dance to bring about particular effects and create particular images.

Aesthetic Judgments Rely on Descriptive Reasons

There are three kinds of descriptive reasons to be considered by viewers in the formulation of their aesthetic judgments. These are described by David Perkins (1981) as *where* reasons, pinpointing a particular part of the work; *what* reasons, describing an aspect or quality of the pinpointed part of the work; and *why* reasons, justifying the evaluative conclusions one draws from where and what reasons by referring to one's critical standards or assumptions (p. 106). These critical standards and assumptions then become subject to assessment; they must be relevant to the particular work under review.

The following examples illustrate the use of these three kinds of reasons in a critical discussion of a dance. One viewer might say "The beginning of the dance is very impressive," which pinpoints where the critical statement is directed. Another viewer might remark "The first several gestures are very clear," which describes what aspect of the beginning of the dance is being considered. A third viewer may add that "The work's originality makes it very strong," which indicates why the work is judged favorably. (Again, the relevance of the stated criterion—in this case originality—may also be discussed; viewers may disagree both on the meaning of the term and on whether it is an important quality in a dance.)

It should also be noted that some critical remarks may include more than one of these three kinds of descriptive reasons. For example, where, what, and why reasons all occur in the following statement: "In the second section of the dance, the last image is weak because it is too symmetrical. The symmetry makes the image very static." In actual critical discussions, of course, these remarks may be elaborated upon, challenged, supported, or amended.

Aesthetic Judgments Are Not Comparative Judgments

To make and justify aesthetic judgments is clearly different from merely labeling or ranking a dance. Indeed, in ranking a work of art, viewers usually just compare it to other works. But to base the judgment of one work solely on comparisons to another work is to confuse *comparative* judgments with *aesthetic* judgments.

Art educator David W. Ecker (1976) observes that in making a comparative judgment, the viewer must first have in mind a particular basis upon which one work of art is to be estimated as more or less effective than another (p. 130). For example, dances A and B may be compared on the basis of how frequently each work simultaneously activates many areas of the stage space. A judgment of this one aspect of the two dances ostensibly determines which is the "better" dance, depending upon whether the viewer making the judgment believes that simultaneously activating many areas of the stage space makes a dance strong or weak.

The problem with comparative judgments, however, is when one focuses on only one aspect of the two dances as the basis for comparison and the sole criterion for judgment and proceeds to declare that one work is weak in comparison to the other on this basis. This necessarily reduces the first work to less than its aesthetic whole; none of its features except the one being compared are taken into consideration. Substituting a comparative judgment for an aesthetic judgment is to commit what philosopher John Dewey (1934) calls "the reductive fallacy." For Dewey, this

> *results from oversimplification. It exists when some constituent of the work of art is isolated and then the whole is reduced to terms of this single isolated element. (p. 315)*

This is not meant to imply that all comparisons between two dances must be excluded from a critical discussion, only that students' attention should be directed to the potential drawbacks of comparison as the sole basis for judgment.

The Ladder of Aesthetic Inquiry

Once students are beginning to engage in the oral description, analysis, interpretation, and evaluation of the dances seen in class, it is helpful to explain to them how critical discourse in art may be seen as consisting of four distinct levels: criticism, metacriticism, theory, and metatheory. As students learn to recognize how remarks made about a work of art correspond to these levels of discourse, their ability and willingness to engage in a critical discussion will expand rapidly.

A useful tool for understanding the four levels of critical discourse in art is Ecker and Kaelin's (1972, p. 267) ladder of aesthetic inquiry (see Figure 9.1).

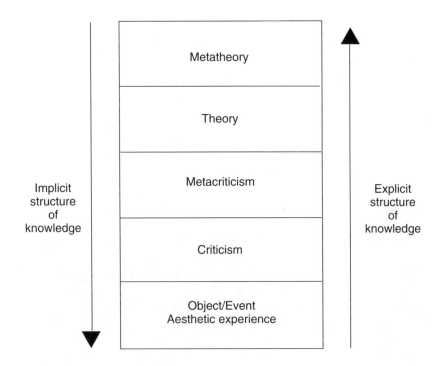

Figure 9.1 The Ecker/Kaelin ladder of aesthetic inquiry.
From "The Limits of Aesthetic Inquiry: A Guide to Educational Research" by David W. Ecker and Eugene F. Kaelin. *Philosophical Redirection of Educational Research,* p. 267, 1972. Reprinted by permission.

The ladder organizes the kinds of claims that can be made about a particular work of art. The aesthetic object or event's location at the bottom of the ladder indicates that all statements associated with any of the "rungs"—or levels—must be relevant to the work under review.

Criticism

When students begin to articulate and debate the contents of their reflective notes during critical discussion and extend these into interpretations and aesthetic judgments of the dance, all descriptive, analytical, interpretive, and evaluative remarks that refer to visible features of the dance occupy the rung of *criticism.* For example, all of the remarks below are examples of critical remarks having directly to do with one or more visible features of the dance.

> **Juan:** *"Six dancers emerged from the upstage right corner and ran quickly to the center of the stage, where they fell to the floor in a circle." (description)*
>
> **Heidi:** *"The movements of the two men were partially obscured by the three women directly in front of them." (analysis; describes a relationship among the dancers)*
>
> **Kate:** *"The arm and hand gestures of the woman in blue clearly represented her sorrow at the departure of the woman in green." (interpretation; describes the significance of part of the work)*
>
> **Tracy:** *"The slow movements used in the transition between the two solos weakened the dance by reducing the excitement that had been generated by the first soloist." (judgment; describes what is evaluated, where it occurred, and why it is judged to be weak)*

The distinction between *exploratory* and *argumentative* criticism is illustrated by the four critical remarks above. The first two are exploratory remarks about the visible features of the dance; they state facts about the work. The referential adequacy of these remarks— i.e., the adequacy with which they describe or analyze the visible properties of the dance—can be relatively easily checked by reflecting on the dance or by seeing it again.

The second two remarks, while having the same grammatical form as exploratory factual claims, are argumentative claims because they draw interpretive and evaluative conclusions about the dance. Argumentative claims such as these, if challenged, rely upon the support of further descriptive and analytical evidence to persuade. Metacritical remarks seek to elicit such further evidence.

Metacriticism

Moving up the ladder, remarks that challenge or support the underlying assumptions or the descriptive accuracy of a critical claim correspond to the rung of *metacriticism*. Both exploratory descriptive and analytical remarks, such as those made by Juan and Heidi, and argumentative interpretive or evaluative claims, such as those made by Kate and Tracy, may be addressed through metacritical remarks. For example, Erik might correct Juan's statement by pointing out that there were not six dancers, but only five. Similarly, a metacritical response to Tracy's judgment that the transition between the two solos weakens the dance might be met with this metacritical response from Holly: "I agree that the transition between the two solos was weak, but I do not think it was simply because the movements were slow. I think the transition was uninteresting because the body design was entirely symmetrical, with no variations."

With these remarks, Holly both supports Tracy's judgment that the transition was weak and adds a critical claim of her own having to do with the symmetry of the body design in the section of the dance in question. It is quite appropriate for metacritical remarks like Holly's to introduce new critical claims while addressing previous ones.

Very often, the function of metacritical remarks is to seek clarification of previous critical claims. For example, suppose Linda says she found the dance to be poorly structured. A metacritical response to this remark from Jeff might ask Linda to say specifically where the structure of the dance is poor. If Linda can provide such a statement, it will show precisely what it is about the structure of the dance she thinks is poor. If she cannot pinpoint a specific part of the work and replies only that the structure is poor because it seems boring, a second metacritical response might assert that "boring" is a pejorative term that merely reiterates her judgment without saying anything substantive about the dance. Moreover, it might be pointed out that Linda has given a why reason for her judgment without providing a corresponding where or what reason. The foregoing illustrates both that why reasons must be supported by where and what reasons, and that the aim of metacritical discourse is to clarify or amend any critical claims that are not warranted by the visible evidence. Developing metacritical skills requires viewers to focus equally on becoming good observers of the dances seen in class and on listening carefully to the critical language of their peers.

Teaching Hints

Although the levels of discourse—criticism, metacriticism, theory, and metatheory—are conceptually distinct, many remarks in a critical discussion will naturally contain ideas belonging to more than one level. It is not necessary to interrupt discussions so that each statement's position on the ladder can be determined. Rather, introduce the ladder to students as a tool for understanding the various kinds of statements viewers can make about a work of art. If a statement in a critical discussion is vague or ambiguous, it can be helpful to identify where on the ladder the statement would appropriately be placed.

An important distinction viewers need to become familiar with is that between *general* and *specific* claims. Because general critical claims tend to be sweeping and usually fail to include adequate support, it is essential to probe them for the specific details upon which they may be based. For example, suppose Neil makes the general assertion that "The performance of the dance was rather sloppy." The simple metacritical question, "How exactly was the performance sloppy?" should be directed to him to try to elicit more specifics (where and what reasons), such as "Jerome dropped his mask and Liz missed her entrance." Interestingly, elaborations such as these upon general claims may themselves take on a metacritical function, subverting, for example, Mark's general assertion that "The dance was well performed."

Theory and Metatheory

Discussion of creative strategies, critical approaches, and general criteria for judgment that might be employed to support various critical and metacritical statements about the dance under review corresponds to the rung of *theory*. For example, Lori's claim that "All good dances clearly communicate some message to the audience" and Carol's claim that "slowing down the movement in the last section of a dance is a good way to make a poignant ending" represent specific theoretical positions. Lori's remark reflects the theoretical position that a dance is a kind of linguistic communication and that it is reasonable to judge a dance on the basis of how clearly its message is communicated. Carol's remarks reflect her theory that slow movement at the end of dances makes them more successful.

During a critical discussion, theoretical remarks such as these must not be accepted at face value, for they are views, not facts, about art. Moreover, to be relevant to the discussion of a particular dance, such theoretical views as these must point directly to or somehow improve viewers' perception of the visible features of the dance under review.

Accordingly, the aim of *metatheoretical* remarks is to identify and support or challenge the underlying assumptions, clarity, or relevance of theoretical claims in exactly the same way that metacritical remarks support or challenge critical claims. For example, Jessica might respond to Lori's theoretical claim that all good dances clearly communicate some message to the audience by pointing out that some works of art have nothing to do with communicating a message and that communication is not a defining characteristic of art in general or of dance specifically. Similarly, Kerry might respond to Carol's claim about the virtues of slowing down the movement at the end of a dance by pointing out that no single choreographic device will work every time because each dance is unique.

Each "higher" rung, or level, of aesthetic discourse, then, refers to one or more of the levels beneath it, and all aesthetic discourse must be directly relevant to the observable features of the particular work—the aesthetic object or event that grounds the discussion at the base of the ladder.

THINK ON IT
Ideas for Writing and Discussion

Find a review or critique of a work of art in a newspaper or magazine. Are judgments clearly made? Are they supported with where, what, and why reasons? If comparative judgments are made, are the bases of comparison clearly stipulated? Are general claims supported with specific ones? Write a short note to the author whose review you have studied. Using your metacritical and metatheoretical skills, let the author know how his or her review is successful or how it might be improved (you do not have to send the note).

Summary: Important Points to Remember

1. A judgment is not a guess, a fact, or a feeling about a work of art. Instead, a judgment is a description of a work's merit or flaws as perceived by the viewer.

2. Aesthetic judgments rely for support upon clearly stated where, what, and why reasons.

3. Because they tend to focus on one aspect of a work rather than upon the work as a whole, comparative judgments should be avoided during critical discussions.

4. Critical discourse in art consists of criticism, metacriticism, theory, and metatheory. Understanding how remarks made in response to a work of art correspond to these levels of discourse will help you to participate more fully in a critical discussion.

Chapter 10

RECOMMENDATIONS FOR REVISIONS

This chapter will help you understand

- the process of critical projection, in which viewers mentally envision how suggestions for revising the dance might affect the work,

- how to make discussion of implemented revisions useful to the choreographer whose dance is under review, and

- the importance of deferring the recommendation of revisions until after interpretive and evaluative discussion.

Choreography courses are structured both to permit and to encourage immediate revision of works presented. Therefore, the final step in the critical process is the recommendation of viewers' choreographic suggestions for the work under review.

Critical Projection

In considering recommended revisions, the students should envision how each proposed change to the dance might affect the work as a whole. In effect, each suggested revision must be mentally "projected" onto the dance. This process is termed *critical projection.*

Critical projection should begin only after all the viewers' interpretive and evaluative claims have been explored and the choreographer has learned which aspects of the dance "worked" for the viewers and which aspects they think need further attention. The shift from the discussion of various judgments to the offering of specific recommendations for revisions usually occurs quite naturally. However, if evaluative discussion appears to have run its course or if it seems to be stalling, it is appropriate for the teacher to invite the group to turn its attention to the suggestion of possible revisions to the dance.

For a choreographer whose work is under review, the critical projection stage presents an opportunity to brainstorm with other choreographers on how best to approach the next period in the development of the dance. Specific choreographic choices and broader aesthetic issues with which the choreographer has thus far been working alone are often clarified through the process of giving careful consideration to the critical projections of others.

Teaching Hints

Occasionally, evaluative discussions become focused on theoretical points related to the relevance and application of specific criteria of judgment. Such shifts in focus can be stimulating to the students or they can become highly abstract and completely disconnected from the actual business of the class—to evaluate the work under review. In the latter cases, the number of active participants in the discussion tends to drop sharply. Use your judgment to determine when your students would benefit from a change in focus, initiated by you, to the recommendation of revisions for the dance.

Recommending Revisions Versus "Fixing" the Dance

It is important to remind viewers that the opportunity to recommend revisions is not an invitation merely to "fix" another's dance. Ultimately, the qualitative character and organization of a work can be revised only by the artist. Neither is the aim of critical projection to achieve a consensus among the viewers on which proposed revisions ought to be implemented. The aim, rather, is to allow the choreographer to hear a variety of substantive critical suggestions. The critical projection stage of the discussion is a gift to the choreographer. The suggestions for revisions, like all evaluative comments, are intended to facilitate rather than to interfere with the choreographer's artistic and aesthetic development.

While viewers are articulating their recommendations for revision, choreographers should be encouraged both to question the comments of the viewers and to suggest their own solutions to perceived problems in the dance. For their part, viewers need to be precise both in identifying the part of the dance for which they would like to recommend a change and in explaining how their proposed revision might affect the dance. For example, the suggestion to "Slow down the movements and change the facing of the soloist in the second section so we can see her face more clearly" is more specific and, therefore, more useful to a choreographer than the general recommendation to "Do something to make the solo part more interesting." Similarly, the suggestion that "The movement motifs and spatial patterns in all of the sections need to be made more clear" gives a choreographer much more to work with than the recommendation to "Tighten up the structure of the dance."

Post-Revision Review

After specific revisions to a dance have been proposed and their merits debated, the choreographer integrates into the dance those suggestions he or she found most useful. Some revisions may be implemented immediately, but others may require time outside of class to be implemented.

When revisions are implemented immediately and the viewers know which suggestions are to be tried, the second viewing of the dance is followed by reflection on and discussion of the revisions' impact on the dance.

If revisions are implemented outside of the class, the second viewing of the dance is followed by repetition of reflective description and analysis. Reflective notes should again be verbalized to determine anew which aspects of each viewer's private experience of the dance may be designated as shared experience. The choreographer should respond to the reflective observations of the viewers by sharing perspectives on the dance as a whole, the nature of the revisions made to it, the manner in which these revisions were implemented, and artistic insights that may have been gained through the creative and critical processes.

In discussing a revised dance, viewers may wish to draw specific comparisons between the original dance and the revised version, comparing and discussing the two versions based on the criteria associated with the implemented revisions. For example, Bob may elect to speed up the movements in a certain section of his dance in response to Joan's judgment that the slowness of the movement in that section breaks the wonderful mood of excitement established by the work's earlier sections. When Bob shows the revised dance with the section in question performed faster than it was before, it is appropriate for the group to consider whether the excitement of the dance has been maintained.

It is important to note that evaluation of the revised dance is to be based neither on the choreographer's success at implementing spe-

cific revisions nor on comparisons of the revised dance with the original version. This means that while Bob may have implemented Joan's
suggestion perfectly, he and the group must now consider whether
the change compromised or weakened some other quality of the
work. For example, has the strong contrast among sections of the
dance that was created in the original version by their different movement speeds now disappeared? If so, what is the effect of this loss of
contrast on the dance as a whole? Is this loss more or less important
than what has been achieved by implementing Joan's suggested revision? These kinds of questions illustrate the importance of evaluating
the revised dance as a unique entity.

Structuring the post-revisions discussion in this manner helps all
the students to discover the valuable contribution to creative efforts
that results from careful and precise critical evaluation. This final stage
of the discussion may include new interpretations and judgments of
the dance by any of the participants, including the choreographer.
But it must again be stressed that the choreographer's artistic intentions in or interpretations of the dance are not more valid than those
of the viewers.

The Importance of Deferring Revision Recommendations

Deferring suggestion of revisions until after interpretations and evaluations have been discussed allows choreographers a chance to reflect
on and respond to descriptive, analytical, interpretive, and evaluative
claims before turning their attention to specific suggestions for revision that grow out of concerns that may be meaningful only to the
viewers. Moreover, this approach teaches choreographers to place all
critical feedback in the proper perspective—to see it as information
about others' responses to the work. Choreographers must examine
this feedback to determine which remarks address what they see as
legitimate problems with the work.

It is easier for choreographers to entertain recommendations for
revisions after they have heard discussion of the strengths or weaknesses others see in the work. As art educator David Perkins (1977, p.
299) has pointed out, until an artist clearly understands others' reasons for suggestions, proposed ideas for revision will likely fall on
deaf ears and may even provoke defensiveness on the part of the
artist toward all evaluative remarks.

There is an additional reason for recommending revisions only after interpretive and evaluative discussion of a dance. It is crucial that viewers experience each dance fully as it is initially presented, resisting the tendency to mentally re-choreograph each dance while watching the performance or to immediately formulate their interpretations, judgments, or suggestions for revision. Viewers need time to focus on reflective description and analysis and to discuss interpretations and judgments of the work before considering how the dance might be improved.

Teaching Hints

Perkins mentions the following defensive rebuttals artists often make to evaluative comments: "Only the expert is good enough to criticize me" and "I want to be judged by my own standards" (p. 299). If student choreographers respond in this manner to evaluation or recommendations for revision of their work, remind them that the comments of their peers are intended only to help them understand their own work better. Remind them also that while artists must sort out what seems to them sound or unsound in a critique, defensiveness blocks open-minded consideration of others' remarks and may prevent even praise from benefiting an artist's future creative efforts.

THINK ON IT
Ideas for Writing and Discussion

Imagine that you have just shown your dance in class. After a period of reflection during which you note your assessments of the work and its performance and your classmates focus on describing and analyzing the visible properties of the work, you await the evaluations of your peers. The first remarks you hear tell you what is "wrong" with your dance and begin to list ways that you should "fix" it. How does this kind of feedback make you feel? How receptive are you to the suggestions you are receiving when you have not yet even heard any discussion of what the viewers noticed in the work?

Summary: Important Points to Remember

1. Critical projection is the mental envisioning of possible revisions for the dance and discussion of how each proposed revision might affect the dance as a whole.

2. The recommendation of revisions should begin only after all the viewers' interpretive and evaluative claims have been explored and the choreographer has learned which aspects of the dance "worked" for the viewers and which aspects they think need further attention.

3. The opportunity to recommend revisions is not an invitation merely to "fix" another's dance. Ultimately, the qualitative character and organization of a work can be revised only by the artist.

PART III

Implementation of the ORDER Approach

The next two chapters are primarily for choreography teachers introducing their students to substantive critical evaluation using the ORDER approach. Student readers who seek greater understanding of the pedagogical issues surrounding critical evaluation in the choreography class will gain valuable insights from these chapters as well.

Chapter 11 focuses on important differences between beginning- and advanced-level choreography courses and offers practical suggestions for implementing the ORDER approach with students at each level.

Chapter 12 addresses common linguistic and rhetorical obstacles teachers may encounter as they introduce the practice of critical evaluation to students. Practical suggestions for overcoming these obstacles are provided.

Following chapter 12 is a brief Afterword which discusses ideas about how students' critical performance might be assessed.

Chapter 11

Skill Level Distinctions in Choreography Courses

This chapter will help you understand

- the differences between beginning- and advanced-level choreography assignments, and
- how to implement the ORDER approach to critical evaluation in beginning- and advanced-level choreography classes.

Choreography courses are generally structured according to students' levels of experience and development. Dance educators ordinarily require beginning-level students to create short "studies" that isolate and explore such individual elements and concepts of dance as body shape, floor pattern, and speed, and fundamental principles of composition such as theme and variation, contrast, and repetition. Thus, while one cannot create a dance study dealing with energy in movement, for example, without also dealing with issues of time and space, each of these elements ordinarily is introduced and explored separately at the beginning level of training. Concentrating beginners' attention on one specific aspect of dance composition at a time enables them both to explore individual elements and concepts and to develop an understanding of the aesthetic possibilities of each element and concept.

Typical Choreography Assignments for Beginners

Improvisational exercises and creative assignments for beginners are generally quite precise about the particular choreographic element or concept to be explored. For example, an assignment prescribed early on by choreography teachers Lynne Anne Blom and L. Tarin Chaplin (1982) introduces the idea of moving in relation to the impulses created by three types of breathing—deep breathing, panting, and deep inhalation with sharp exhalation. This assignment reads as follows:

> *Create a study based on breath. Include all three types of breathing, using the breath audibly throughout. All movements should be breath instigated. Perform twice, with and without the audible breathing. (p. 25)*

Similarly, after introducing the concepts of symmetry and asymmetry, students are assigned to:

> *Create a study using symmetry and asymmetry. At some point combine the nonaffinities (e.g., move in symmetry and hold positions in asymmetry, or have tensions in symmetry and calm authority in asymmetry). (p. 41)*

Both assignments present a choreographic problem that isolates a single artistic element or concept. The dance studies created in response to this kind of assignment are, therefore, not full or complete dances. Rather, their purpose is to develop each choreographer's understanding of a single compositional element.

Beginning-level assignments such as these imply a clear criterion for assessing the results of each choreographer's creative efforts. For example, the studies students produce in response to the breathing assignment may appropriately be evaluated on the basis of how clearly each student utilizes the three kinds of breathing prescribed and on the clarity with which the movements are breath instigated. Thus, while each student's study will be unique, it is a relatively routine matter for an observer to recognize the ways it addresses the assigned choreographic issue.

Presented and Discovered Problems

The two sample choreography assignments demonstrate that at the beginning level of choreography training, the creative process involves responding to a problematic situation. All creative problem-solving situations consist of three phases. Educational theorists Jacob W. Getzels and Mihaly Csikszentmihalyi (1976, p. 79) describe these three phases as

1. the formulation of a problem,
2. the adoption of a method of solution, and
3. the reaching of a solution.

However, the authors also point out that while all problem situations may share these three basic elements,

> *At one extreme there are presented problem situations where the problem has a known formulation, a routine method of solution,*

*and a recognized solution; here a person need only follow estab-
lished steps to meet the requirements of the situation. At the other
extreme there are* discovered problem situations . . . *here the
person must identify the problem itself, and there are no
established steps for satisfying the requirements of the situation.
(p. 79)*

Applying these concepts to choreography training and recalling
the two sample choreography assignments just reviewed, it's clear
that beginning-level class sessions provide students with presented
problem situations, in which fairly routine approaches to a problem
and easily recognized solutions dominate.

The ORDER approach to critical evaluation should be implemented
in abbreviated form in beginning-level classes because these students
usually produce frequent short dance studies focusing mainly upon
presented problems related to the mastery of individual design elements. At this level, critical evaluation may appropriately consist of
observation, reflective description and analysis, and the sharing of
reflective notes.

In introducing the ORDER approach to beginning choreography
students, it is important to emphasize the necessity for attentive, open-
minded viewing of each dance. As dance critic Marcia Siegel (1981)
puts it:

*Dance is not just arms and legs moving, not just entrances and
exits. It is movement with form and expression. We can learn to
see, in the split second of its occurrence, the unfolding structure
of movement, the kind of phrasing and rhythms, the effect of
changing the way people are situated in a stage space, what happens when movement slows down or speeds up, the habitual patterns of gesture and impulse that make for style. . . . In the watching, immediacy and openness, the sensory system . . . and a rather
elemental use of the wits are called for. (p. 21)*

It is also important to consolidate observations into clear and detailed reflective notes. The ensuing discussion can then focus on the
students' perceptions of the particular choreographic element, concept, or problem upon which an assignment has been based. Thus,
the focus of critical discussion at the beginning level is consideration
of how each choreographer has addressed the problem presented in
each assignment.

Critical Projection With Beginners

A variant of critical projection, which was discussed earlier (chapter 10) in conjunction with the recommendation of revisions, can be introduced to beginning-level students as preliminary work in interpreting and evaluating dances.

In beginning-level choreography courses, a different kind of critical projection facilitates critical discussions of the studies produced in response to a choreographic problem. Seeing some or all of the studies again, in whole or in part, is the best stimulus to critical projection at the beginning level. Seeing a dance study performed a second time promotes precise observation and deeper reflection by the students. Rather than viewing simple studies merely as one-time learning exercises designed to work out a specific problem, students come to see them as revealing and illuminating new choreographic possibilities.

You can initiate critical projection with beginning-level students by asking them to reflect on all of the studies just seen and to speculate as to how two or more of them might be combined; or how a particular study might be developed or be incorporated as is into a larger and more complex dance. Looking at beginning-level exercises in this way helps students to appreciate the relationship between developmental studies in choreographic craft and complex, mature dances.

Critical projection with beginners encourages students to engage in theoretical discussions about the ways individual choreographic elements and concepts might be employed, alone or in conjunction with other elements and concepts that have already been explored in earlier assignments, to create more complex choreographic forms and meanings.

Theoretical discussions of this kind focus students' reflective attention upon formal or expressive properties of various works that, because they were not directly relevant to the choreographic problem addressed by the study, may not previously have been identified and discussed. For example, during the second performance of a study that was created and observed specifically to stimulate students' understanding of the negative and positive space created by the dancer's changing body shapes, a dancer's speed and energy dynamics may also be noticed by the viewers. The class as a whole might then turn to creating studies based on energy dynamics in order to explore this newly discovered artistic element further.

Through critical projection, beginning students discover relationships between artistic form and meaning by discussing how particular meanings can attach themselves to structured movement without the choreographer's necessarily having intended this to happen. Because all claims made during critical projection must refer directly to the visible features of one or more of the studies just seen, critical projection teaches beginning students the difference between experiencing meaning in a dance and reading meaning into a dance. This, in turn, provides teachers with an opportunity to introduce the idea of artistic ambiguity. Finally, engaging in critical projection helps students learn to move beyond purely subjective responses and toward detailed description in critical evaluation.

The ORDER Approach in Beginning-Level Classes

Observation:
- Attend carefully to each work seen.
- Focus on noticing how the dance "works."

Reflection:
- Describe and analyze movements, gestures, motifs, patterns, and their interrelationships.

Discussion:
- Focus on the way the assigned choreographic concept or problem has been handled in the dance.
- Use critical projection to discover how individual choreographic elements and concepts might be employed alone or in conjunction with previously explored elements and concepts to create more complex choreographic forms and meanings.

Typical Choreography Assignments for Advanced Students

Advanced-level choreography courses prompt students' creative efforts with increasingly open-ended assignments, allowing choreographers not only to select and incorporate previously isolated elements and principles, but also inviting them to develop and work with themes, ideas, concepts, and intuitions drawn from any domain.

In assignments intended for advanced students, choreographic elements and concepts previously isolated in beginning-level assignments are combined. For example, Blom and Chaplin (1982) assign students to

> *Choreograph a study highlighting a variety of movements or uti-*
> *lizing various ways of highlighting one movement. Be careful*
> *not to have so much highlighting that it takes over and becomes*
> *the dominant content. (p. 108)*

Later, the authors propose that students

> *Find a single article that could be used as costume, prop, and set.*
> *Improvise with it in all ways. Choreograph a short piece that capi-*
> *talizes on its versatility. (p. 195)*

In contrast to the presented-problem assignments for beginning-level choreography students, these assignments present comparatively open-ended choreographic problems: to highlight one or many movements in a variety of ways and to improvise with a prop "in all ways." Dance studies produced for these assignments will be wider in scope and, therefore, more challenging to evaluate than the two beginning-level studies because criteria for recognizing success at the advanced level are not delineated by the assignment itself. Highlighting movements in a variety of ways, while still an exercise in surface design, is an open-ended choreographic problem compared to the beginning-level studies. The highlighting assignment is, therefore, likely to generate a greater variety of choreographic results than the first two assignments. Moreover, in viewing and reflecting on the resulting studies, different aspects of the movements may be perceived by different observers as constituting the highlights the choreographer has included in the dance.

Similarly, the prop assignment, which calls for students to improvise with a single prop or article, offers students an even wider range of artistic choices and possible actions as they create not just short studies, but actual dances. The assignment requires only that an object of some kind be utilized. In creating dances responding to this stipulation, students are free to consciously incorporate any of the choreographic elements and concepts isolated in previous exercises. But because the problem this assignment is based on allows students to expand beyond a limited exploration of surface design elements, discussion of the dances produced is likely to venture beyond basic description and analysis and toward critical interpretation and evaluation of artistic meaning(s) and aesthetic value.

Discovered-Problem Situations

As the examples of the highlighting and prop assignments show, assignments given to students in advanced choreography courses are actually discovered-problem situations. In discovered-problem situations, students are asked to respond to open-ended prompts, formulate their own artistic problems, invent methods of solution, and determine for themselves when solutions have been achieved.

This means that the advanced choreography student must, as Getzels and Csikszentmihalyi (1976) put it,

> *pose the problem before he can begin to think of a way of solving it, and when he reaches a solution—if he reaches it—he has no way of knowing whether it is right or wrong. Not only the solution but the problem itself must be discovered, and when the solution is found, it cannot be compared against a predetermined standard. It can be accepted or rejected only on the basis of a critical, relativistic analysis—as is the case with works of art.* (p. 82)

As students begin to work on discovered-problem assignments, it is appropriate to implement the latter stages of the ORDER approach—interpretation and evaluation, the recommendation of revisions, and post-revisions review. The work students have done in their beginning-level classes on observing, describing, analyzing, and discussing dances will have prepared them well for these latter stages of the ORDER approach.

The ORDER Approach in Advanced-Level Classes

Observation:
- Attend carefully to each work seen.
- Focus on noticing how the dance "works."

Reflection:
- Describe and analyze movements, gestures, motifs, patterns, and their interrelationships.

Discussion:
- Share reflective descriptions and analyses of the visible properties of the work.
- Articulate interpretations of the meaning or significance of the work.

Evaluation:	• Articulate evaluations of the aesthetic merit of the work.
Revisions:	• Suggest or demonstrate recommended revisions for the dance.
	• Use critical projection to assess the aesthetic impact of suggested revisions on the dance as a whole.
	• Assess implemented revisions.

Summary: Important Points to Remember

1. The ORDER approach to critical evaluation is designed for both beginning- and advanced-level choreography courses. The first three steps—observation, reflection, and the initial stage of discussion—are recommended for beginning-level courses. In these courses, students respond to presented problems by creating brief dances to demonstrate their grasp of a particular concept or choreographic principle.

2. A period of critical projection during which students discuss possibilities for further developing one or more of the dances already seen is recommended for beginning-level courses.

3. As students progress in their training toward creating more elaborate dances that embody a variety of concepts and principles of dance, it is appropriate to introduce the latter steps of the ORDER approach—the evaluative stage of discussion, the recommendation of revisions, and the post-revisions review. At this point in their training, the experience students have gained in observing, describing, analyzing, and discussing dances will have prepared them well for these latter stages of the ORDER approach.

Chapter 12

POTENTIAL OBSTACLES TO CRITICAL EVALUATION

This chapter will help you understand

- how to overcome students' anticritical beliefs and attitudes,
- how to handle critical disagreements that arise during class discussions of a dance, and
- how to overcome common linguistic and rhetorical causes of apparent disagreement.

An important pedagogical issue in critical evaluation is students' initial lack of familiarity with even the basic critical skills necessary to evaluate works of art and their consequent reluctance to engage in critical discussions either of their own work or that of their peers. It is worthwhile to briefly consider common pitfalls that choreography teachers may encounter as they introduce critical evaluation to their students. Familiarity with these pitfalls and effective ways to deal with them will make implementation of the ORDER approach easier for teachers and more rewarding for students.

Even when they observe attentively, students beginning to confront the wide array of choreographic elements and their relationships may experience trouble distinguishing them. Students may find it difficult, as well, to describe and analyze these elements' appearance in a particular work.

Handling Anticritical Beliefs and Attitudes

The difficulties outlined above may be aggravated for some students by unconscious or previously unexamined anticritical beliefs and attitudes. Six common anticritical attitudes are listed below. (The chapter numbers immediately following each item on the list indicate where in this book the philosophical issues relevant to each belief are discussed. It may be helpful to require students holding these beliefs to review, write about, and discuss these sections of the text.)

1. Some students may believe that simply describing and analyzing the features of a work of art reveals nothing significant about the work and that art speaks directly to one's feelings and can be reacted to only on the subjective level. These students will tend to articulate only subjective responses to the

dances seen in class rather than concentrate on describing the work's aesthetic properties. See chapter 2.

2. During interpretive discussion, students may invent stories about the work of art rather than focus on the expressive character of its visible properties. These students will usually have difficulty articulating the connections between their interpretations and the visible properties of the works seen in class. See chapter 8.

3. Students may cling vigorously to the notion that the task of interpretation is to discover the one "message" the artist is trying to communicate to the viewers. Instead of formulating their own interpretations of the works seen in class, these students will likely ask choreographers for explanations of the meanings of their works and regard choreographers' interpretations as definitive. See chapter 4.

4. In evaluating such aspects of a dance as the choreographer's choice of movements, the structuring of formal elements in relation to subject matter, or the execution of the choreography by the dancers, student critics may have trouble recognizing the difference between liking a work and assessing its aesthetic value. These students will probably employ such phrases as "I liked it" and "I could relate to the feelings in that dance" as reasons for their aesthetic judgments. See chapter 2 and chapter 9.

5. Students may resist the idea that making aesthetic judgments necessitates description and the support of relevant reasons. These students will tend to have difficulty articulating the connections between their evaluations and the visible properties of the works seen in class. See chapter 9.

6. Students may think that the absence of universally applicable criteria makes futile any attempts to evaluate works of art. These students will rarely share their evaluations of the works seen in class, and may even insist that "There is no way to judge art, so why bother talking about it?" See chapter 3.

Teachers should not be discouraged by the manifestation of these beliefs among their students. As students develop—through reading, writing, and discussion—an understanding of each step of the OR-DER approach to critical evaluation and have opportunities to use the approach in their choreography classes, they quickly see the valuable contribution that substantive critical evaluation makes to their creative efforts.

The Belief that Judgment Is Imposition

One very common anticritical belief deserves special consideration—the belief that an aesthetic judgment amounts to little more than the unwarranted imposition of one's personal artistic preferences on others. Students with this belief will prefer not to articulate evaluations of others' dances. If asked why they are silent during evaluative discussions, they will often reply that "Nobody likes to have their work judged" or that "It is not my place to judge my friend's work."

Like the other anticritical beliefs and attitudes mentioned previously, the belief that judgment is imposition is characteristic of students who do not understand how judgments differ from guesses, feelings, facts, and recommendations for revisions (see chapter 9). Once the proper role of judgment in the critical process is made clear through working with the ORDER approach, participation in the critical process becomes more comfortable for these students.

Self-Censorship

The belief that judgment is imposition often leads to self-censorship on the part of student viewers. Students who self-censor their evaluative comments usually do so to protect the feelings of the choreographer whose work is under review.

While it is true that students' self-censoring may contribute to a smoother critical discussion, for example, by reducing the risk of perceived insult, it also reduces the flow of information. Choreographers need to hear the critical opinions of their peers to understand how their dances might be improved. After all, the choreography class is a creative learning laboratory in which all the participants seek to develop their dance-making skills.

To overcome the tendency of some students to self-censor their critical remarks and to make sure students fully understand the importance of delivering their critical feedback to the artist whose work is under review, choreography teachers should ensure that students comprehend each stage of the ORDER approach and the rationale for structuring critical evaluation according to this approach. It is not sufficient to quickly introduce the approach on the first day of class and expect that students will immediately be able to utilize it.

Each step of the ORDER approach is intended to be introduced, implemented, and discussed before proceeding to the next step. In this way, students will learn both how to do critical evaluation and why it is important to do it in a systematic way. Teachers should keep in mind that any awkwardness or difficulty students may experience as they learn how to evaluate dances is not a pedagogical problem or a failing of teaching or learning. The primary objective of the choreography course, after all, is for students to create dances; exercises and assignments leading directly to the creation of dances will occupy most of the students' time. It should not be expected, therefore, that students will demonstrate or attain a professional level of competence as critics.

As students become familiar with the basic skills of criticism—description, analysis, interpretation, and judgment—and with the levels of discourse on the ladder of aesthetic inquiry, the kinds of misconceptions that can provoke reluctance to engage in critical evaluation will begin to fade. Grounding critical evaluation (at all levels of choreography training) in attentive observation and reflection leads students quickly to discover that critical discourse, no matter how awkward it may seem at first, can indeed improve their perception of works of art. In addition, as students profit from increasingly perceptive peer criticism and learn to provide this to others, they come to recognize the positive influence of giving and receiving critical evaluation on their creative endeavors.

Handling Critical Disagreements

Once students are actively engaged in the systematic critical evaluation of dances seen in the choreography class, some fairly vigorous debates inevitably take place in the classroom. Differences of opinion among viewers can arise during discussion, for example, over the aptness of an interpretation or the relevance of evidence offered in support of a judgment. When disagreements arise among the participants of a critical discussion, the teacher should avoid taking the position of decisive critical authority—such disagreements are not settled by a teacher's stating who is "right." Rather, these situations present two questions: Are differences of opinion a genuine pedagogical problem? Must all disagreements be settled?

Is Disagreement a Problem?

Seeing disagreements that arise during critical discussions as a pedagogical problem may lead some teachers to play down the inherently argumentative nature of the interpretive and evaluative stages of the critical process. This can be appropriate to some degree, since there is no pedagogical requirement that the class as a whole pursue critical discussion toward, or prolong it to the point of, achieving a group consensus. But just as total critical agreement is not the goal of class discussions, there is no reason to avoid natural critical disagreements. Each viewer must endeavor both to arrive at and to argue the merits of his or her own conclusions.

Must Critical Disagreements Be Settled?

Before turning to the question of whether critical disagreements must be settled when they arise in choreography classes and other pedagogical settings, it is necessary first to distinguish between genuine and false disagreements.

Genuine disagreement can occur only when at least the possibility of agreement through reasonable argument exists. Clearly, in matters of personal likes and dislikes, one person will not likely change the view of another through argument. In any case, no genuine conflict exists when Bill likes and Don dislikes a particular aspect of a dance.

On the other hand, genuine disagreements do arise between individuals during critical discussions that focus upon the visible features of a work. These disagreements, which may concern such things as the sophistication of a work's design, the aesthetic appropriateness of a particular placement of artistic elements, or the meaning of the work as a whole, are identified, understood, and explored as viewers reflect upon and discuss the work. While such disagreements are sometimes settled as discussion proceeds, it does not follow that the discussion has failed when there is no agreement.

Thus, in the choreography class, discussion of a particular dance need not result in the participants' agreeing how the dance is to be interpreted, judged, or revised or whether enacted revisions have succeeded in bringing about the changes they were intended to produce in the dance. At no time is consensus among the students necessary or even particularly desirable.

What is desirable, however, is clear and relevant critical, metacritical, theoretical, and metatheoretical discourse. The aim of this discourse is for both the choreographer and the viewers to discover precisely how the dance under review is seen, interpreted, and judged by others and to relate the findings of others to their own experiences of the dance. Competing assessments of a dance are therefore best conceived of the way philosopher Morris Weitz (1956) describes competing theories of art—as "seriously made recommendations to attend in certain ways to certain features of art" (p. 35). This means that each competing assessment (or interpretation) of a dance is useful insofar as it suggests a particular way of seeing the dance.

Linguistic and Rhetorical Causes of Disagreement

There are several linguistic and rhetorical triggers for disagreement in critical discussions that educators should keep in mind. In chapter 9, the problem of critics issuing *why* reasons for judgments without corresponding *where* and *what* reasons was discussed along with the problem of general assertions that are unsupported by specifics. David Perkins (1977) outlines a number of other factors that often plague critical discussion:

> *Perhaps one party has missed a consideration, overweighted the evidence, perceived a misleading gestalt. Perhaps generally meaningful terms are being used in contexts where their application is borderline. Perhaps alternative interpretations or perceptions are equally supported by the work. In this case the "reality" of the situation is the ambiguity of the work; apprehending it as it is calls for acknowledging that ambiguity. (p. 290)*

The Problem of Talking Past One Another

Perkins goes on to delineate a problem inherent in the structure of critical dialogue that can create the impression that disagreement exists where there really is none, thereby stalling critical discourse. Using drama as an example, he writes:

> *First and most simply, people talk past one another. One may say, 'I was impressed by the acting,' where another answers, 'But look, the plot makes no sense at all.' One has given a point favoring, the other criticizing the work, and certainly accumulating such points contributes to a comprehensive appraisal. But the second has not indicated whether or not he agrees with the initial remark. (p. 294)*

The problem of critics talking past one another may be avoided by familiarizing students with the levels of discourse on the ladder of aesthetic inquiry (see chapter 9). Once students understand that critical claims must be supported, corrected, or challenged with metacritical questions or claims, discussions like the one Perkins quotes will not occur. Critical claims such as "I was impressed by the dancing" will be met with metacritical questions and claims such as "What specifically were you impressed by? I found the dancers quite weak."

Three Semantic Problems

Philosopher Bernard C. Heyl (1943) explains three causes of "semantic confusion" contributing to what he terms "the inadequacy of contemporary art criticism and aesthetics" (p. 49). These same three problems—"real" definitions, verbal exaggerations, and verbal vagueness—are likely to plague students' initial attempts to engage in substantive critical discussion.

Definitions.   Heyl contends that many of the terms used by critical observers in evaluating works of art, such as *beauty, truth, value, representation, expression, form, content,* and *style,* are problematic because they

> *are constantly receiving multiple definitions, so that any attempt to find a single precise and preferred usage for them would be in itself a tremendous, if not a hopeless task, and its outcome, because inevitably tentative, would prove to be historically interesting rather than practically fruitful. (p. 16)*

However, it is not uncommon for critical observers to use words such as those listed above as if their meanings were fixed and agreed upon by all. For example, student critics often say such things as "That dancer had great expression"; "I liked the content but the form wasn't very good"; and "The style was the best thing about that dance." When statements like these are made, critical discussions frequently veer off into arguments or puzzlement over the use of certain words in relation to the work under review. To remedy this, Heyl recommends that critics learn to provide what he calls "volitional definitions" for these words; such definitions will both clarify and simplify critical discussion. Elaborating, Heyl distinguishes volitional definitions from propositions:

> *Volitional definitions, in contrast to propositions (or to statements and judgments), are about language; they define words, not things; they do not assert facts, and hence do not raise issues of truth and falsehood. (p. 13)*

This means that in the choreography class, viewers should try to stipulate how they are using general aesthetic terms and should provide volitional definitions for their terms before advancing propositions that depend upon a clear understanding of these terms.

For example, suppose Nora remarks "The style of the dance does not seem appropriate to me." Before posing to Nora the metacritical question, "Appropriate for what?" the group needs her to clarify—i.e., give a volitional definition for—the term "style." The term can refer to mannerisms of performance peculiar to the dancer(s) in the piece, to the way the dance is structured, or to a recognized dance form such as flamenco or classical ballet. Therefore, the best metacritical response one might give to Nora is "What do you mean by style?"

Suppose Nora replies that she means "the abrupt and precise way that the transitions are made between the three sections of the dance." This remark provides the other viewers with specific information about the work and makes it easier for Nora's original claim (that the style did not seem appropriate) to be pursued than it would have been had she not provided a volitional definition for "style."

The practice of listening carefully to each other's critical language and learning to provide volitional definitions will help students appreciate how precise critical language must be if it is to successfully widen others' perception of the work of art. Moreover, students will quickly learn to recognize different ways general aesthetic terms may operate in critical discourse.

Exaggeration.   The second semantic issue Heyl raises is that of verbal exaggeration. According to Heyl, certain words, such as *only*, *merely*, *proper*, *correct*, and *all*, give many sentences an overemphasis that is often misleading. Consider, for example, the italicized words in the following statements: "The meaning of this dance may be understood *only* if one considers . . . "; "*Obviously* the dancer in blue is in *correct* time with . . . "; "The *ultimate* message that this dance communicates is. . . ." The italicized words render the propositions highly questionable and are likely to spark disagreements among viewers rather than promote further reflection on and discussion of the dance.

Vagueness.   The third semantic difficulty Heyl identifies is verbal vagueness. By this he means chiefly that much critical language expresses or arouses emotions without referring "to any specific quality or state of affairs" (p. 45). In a critical discussion of a dance, the problem arises when the dance is called, for example, *splendid, awful*, or *incredible*, without attention to any property of the dance to which these words refer. Such language is more emotive than referential. It is vague rather than precise.

The Remedy for Linguistic and Rhetorical Disagreements

Teachers should listen carefully to the language students use in describing, analyzing, interpreting, evaluating, and discussing revisions for dances. When disagreements due to any of the linguistic and rhetorical problems just discussed arise during a critical discussion, teachers should prompt students to identify the precise meaning of the terms used in critical claims, to explain the degree to which these claims are relevant to the dance itself, and, finally, to articulate specific reasons to justify claims.

Before long, students will begin to ask clarifying questions of one another in an effort to improve their discussions. This process will often dissolve critical disagreements, but if disagreement remains, it means only that no individual way of seeing, interpreting, judging, or talking about the dance has been sufficiently persuasive to lead to consensus. But, as mentioned earlier, the proper focus of critical discussion is not to achieve a consensus. It is, rather, to improve viewers' perception of the work under review, to articulate reasonable interpretations and judgments of it, and thereby to provide student choreographers with substantive and relevant critical feedback.

Summary: Important Points to Remember

1. Teachers should not be discouraged by anticritical beliefs their students may display. As students develop—through reading, writing, and discussion—an understanding of what it means to "see" a dance clearly and deliver precise feedback to the choreographer, they will begin to appreciate the contribution that substantive critical evaluation makes to their own creative efforts.

2. To assure that students fully understand the importance of delivering precise critical feedback to the choreographer whose work is under review, teachers should thoroughly introduce, implement, and discuss with students each step of the ORDER approach.

3. Reaching consensus of opinion in critical discussions is not the goal of these discussions. In fact, there is no reason either to avoid disagreements or pursue them to try to achieve a consensus. Each viewer must endeavor both to arrive at and to argue the merits of his or her own critical conclusions.

4. Linguistic and rhetorical causes of disagreement may be remedied through the use of follow-up questions that help students clarify any ambiguous terms or concepts used in a critical claim.

AFTERWORD

Teachers of the arts often wonder how exactly they should assess students' learning. This is an interesting question in the context of implementing the ORDER approach to critical evaluation in the choreography class. Obviously, the question cannot be answered in a purely quantitative way. Students' success in learning to discuss their dances in a serious and substantive way cannot be measured, for example, by counting how many dances are discussed or noting how long each critical discussion lasts. How, then, should choreography teachers assess whether their students are doing criticism "correctly," or are gaining anything from doing it at all?

The notion of "correctness" has a very limited meaning when applied to the development and exercise of critical thinking skills. Observation, for example, is accomplished "correctly" when it is done with an attitude of perceptual openness toward the work observed, with a mind as free of prejudice and critical assumptions as the critic can achieve. The success of a person's efforts in observation is ultimately revealed by the content of the reflective descriptions and analyses produced, and then only to the degree that these observations refer directly to the visible properties of the work under review.

This criterion for correctness applies to the later stages of a critical discussion as well. The information about the dance contained in the descriptive reasons one gives for one's interpretation, evaluation, and recommendations for revisions might be clear and directly relevant to the work, or it might be unclear and irrelevant. Thus, in all cases, the visible properties of the dance itself provide the standard of correctness for all remarks made about it. This means that students are doing critical evaluation "correctly" when their critical remarks afford a match with the work under review, and help others see and understand the work more clearly.

But what specifically do choreographers gain from doing critical evaluation in the choreography class? The answer to this question is simple: They get better at making dances. Their understanding of how dances work and how they might work better is enriched, and this improves their dance-making skills.

At any given moment, students' dance-making skills lag somewhat behind their intellectual understanding of dance and the choreographic process. Whenever new understanding or insight is achieved, it takes time for this to be manifested in the students' creative work. This is one of the reasons why art-making in general is difficult—one always knows a bit more about what to do than one is capable of doing. It follows that students' art-making skills cannot improve if their understanding remains at a static level. For their skills to increase steadily, understanding of how works of art "work" must increase steadily. The practice of substantive critical evaluation of the dances seen in class improves students' understanding of dances. Students apply their new understanding in their dance-making activities, and their dances improve. This improvement is not abstract or invisible; it may be seen by looking at the works students create. It may be fully understood, and traced directly back to the students' critical practice, by discussing with them the artistic principles and creative strategies they have employed and by examining with them the criteria by which they evaluate their own and others' dances.

Seen in this light, the ORDER approach to critical evaluation is an instrument of empowerment for student artists. Its use in choreography courses strengthens each student's creative and critical voices, which are, in the final analysis, truly one voice within each individual.

BIBLIOGRAPHY

Adams, Hazard, and Leroy Searle, eds. *Critical Theory Since 1965*. Tallahassee: University Presses of Florida, 1986.

———, eds. *Critical Theory Since Plato*. New York: Harcourt Brace Jovanovich, 1971.

Adshead, Janet, et al. "A Chart of Skills and Concepts for Dance." *Journal of Aesthetic Education* 16, no. 3 (1982): 49-61.

Adshead, Janet, Valerie A. Briginshaw, Pauline Hodgens, and Michael Huxley. *Dance Analysis: Theory and Practice*. London: Dance Books, Ltd., 1988.

Aiken, Henry David. "The Aesthetic Relevance of Artists' Intentions." *Journal of Philosophy* 52 (1955): 742-753.

Aldrich, Virgil C. *Philosophy of Art*. Englewood Cliffs, NJ: Prentice-Hall, 1963.

Arnheim, Rudolf. "Perceiving, Thinking, Forming." *Art Education* 36, no. 2 (1983): 9-11.

Auslander, Philip. "Embodiment: The Politics of Postmodern Dance." *The Drama Review* 32, no. 4 (1988): 7-23.

Bamberger, Jeanne, and Donald A. Schon. "Learning as Reflective Conversation with Materials: Notes from Work in Progress." *Art Education* 36, no. 2 (1983): 68-73.

Barrett, Terry. "Description in Professional Art Criticism." *Studies in Art Education* 32, no. 2 (1991): 83-93.

————. "A Consideration of Criticism." *Journal of Aesthetic Education* 23, no. 4 (1989): 23-35.

Barthes, Roland. *Image, Music, and Text.* New York: Noonday Press, 1988: 142-148.

Beardsley, Monroe C. *The Aesthetic Point of View.* Ithaca, NY: Cornell University Press, 1982.

————. *The Possibility of Criticism.* Detroit: Wayne State University Press, 1970.

————. "The Classification of Critical Reasons." *Journal of Aesthetic Education* 2, no. 3 (1968): 55-63.

Beiswanger, George. "Chance and Design in Choreography." In *The Dance Experience,* edited by Myron Howard Nadel and Constance Nadel Miller, 82-89. New York: Universe Books, 1978.

————. "Rakes Progress or Dances and the Critic." *Dance Scope* 10, no. 2 (1976): 29-34.

————. "Doing and Viewing Dance: A Perspective for the Practice of Criticism." *Dance Perspectives* 55 (1973): 8-13.

————. "New London: Residues and Reflections." *Dance Observer* 23, no. 9 (1956): 133-135.

Best, David. *Philosophy and Human Movement.* London: George Allen and Unwin, 1978.

————. "Some Problems in the Aesthetics of Dance." *Journal of Aesthetic Education* 9, no. 3 (1975): 105-111.

Bleich, David. *Subjective Criticism.* Baltimore: Johns Hopkins University Press, 1978.

Blocker, Gene H. "The Oilcan Theory of Criticism." *Journal of Aesthetic Education* 9, no. 4 (1975): 19-28.

Blom, Lynne Anne, and L. Tarin Chaplin. *The Intimate Act of Choreography.* Pittsburgh: University of Pittsburgh Press, 1982.

————. *The Moment of Movement.* Pittsburgh: University of Pittsburgh Press, 1988.

Boas, George. *A Primer for Critics.* Baltimore: Johns Hopkins University Press, 1937.

Brennan, Mary Alice. "On Creativity." *Aesthetics and Dance.* AAHPERD Publications, 1980. 1-3.

Carter, Curtis. "Arts and Cognition: Performance, Criticism, and Aesthetics." *Art Education* 36, no. 2 (1983): 61-67.

————. "Some Notes on Aesthetics and Dance Criticism." *Dance Scope* 10 (1976): 35-39.

Casey, John. *The Language of Criticism.* London: Methuen, 1966.

Cheney, Gay. *Basic Concepts in Modern Dance.* 3rd ed. Pennington, NJ: Princeton Book, 1989.

Clements, Robert D. "The Inductive Method of Teaching Visual Art Criticism." *Journal of Aesthetic Education* 13, no. 3 (1979): 67-78.

Codd, John A. "Interpretive Cognition and the Education of Artistic Appreciation." *Journal of Aesthetic Education* 16, no. 3 (1982): 15-33.

Cohen, Marshall. "Primitivism, Modernism, and Dance Theory." In *What Is Dance?,* edited by Roger Copeland and Marshall Cohen, 161-177. Oxford: Oxford University Press, 1983.

Cohen, Selma Jeanne. "A Prolegomenon to an Aesthetics of Dance." *Journal of Aesthetics and Art Criticism* 21, no. 1 (1962): 19-26.

Coleman, Maratha. "On the Teaching of Choreography: Interview with Alwin Nikolais." *Dance Observer* 17, no. 10 (1950): 148-150.

Collingwood, R.G. *The Principles of Art.* New York: Oxford University Press, 1958.

Crittenden, Brian S. "From Description to Evaluation in Aesthetic Judgment." *Journal of Aesthetic Education* 2, no. 4 (1968): 37-58.

Daly, Ann. "Movement Analysis: Piecing Together the Puzzle." *The Drama Review* 32, no. 4 (1988): 40-52.

Dance: A Projection for the Future. Proceedings of the Developmental Conference on Dance, UCLA, Nov. 24-Dec. 3, 1966 and May 28-June 3, 1967.

Dewey, John. *Art as Experience.* New York: Perigee Books, 1934.

Dickie, George. *Evaluating Art.* Philadelphia: Temple University Press, 1988.

———. "The Myth of the Aesthetic Attitude." In *Philosophy Looks at the Arts,* edited by Joseph Margolis. Philadelphia: Temple University Press, 1987.

Ecker, David W., ed. *Qualitative Evaluation in the Arts.* Proceedings of the First Summer Institute on Qualitative Evaluation in the Arts. New York: New York University Division of Arts and Arts Education, 1980.

———. "The Critical Act in Aesthetic Inquiry." In *The Arts, Human Development, and Education,* edited by Elliot W. Eisner, 111-131. Berkeley: McCutchan Publishing Corporation, 1976.

———. "Teaching Art Criticism as Aesthetic Inquiry." *NYU Education Quarterly* 3, no. 4 (1972): 20-26.

———. "Justifying Aesthetic Judgments." *Art Education* 20 (1967): 5-8.

———. "The Artistic Process as Qualitative Problem Solving." *Journal of Aesthetics and Art Criticism* 21, no. 3 (1963): 283-290.

Ecker, David W., and Terry L. Baker. "Multiple Perception Analysis: A Convergence Model for Evaluating Arts Education." *Studies in Arts Education* 25, no. 4 (1984): 245-250.

Ecker, David W., and Eugene F. Kaelin. "The Limits of Aesthetic Inquiry: A Guide to Educational Research." In *Philosophical Redirection of Educational Research*, edited by Lawrence G. Thomas, 258-286. Chicago: University of Chicago Press, 1972.

Edie, James M. *Edmund Husserl's Phenomenology: A Critical Commentary.* Bloomington: Indiana University Press, 1987.

Eisner, Elliot W. "The Mythology of Art Education." *Curriculum Theory Network* 4, nos. 2-3 (1974): 89-100.

Ellfeldt, Lois. *A Primer For Choreographers.* Prospect Heights, IL: Waveland Press, 1967.

Engel, Martin. "Art and the Mind." *Art Education* 36, no. 2 (1983): 6-8.

Fallico, Arturo B. *Art and Existentialism.* Englewood Cliffs, NJ: Prentice-Hall, 1962.

Feldman, Edmund B. "The Teacher as Model Critic." *Journal of Aesthetic Education* 7, no. 2 (1973): 50-57.

———. *Varieties of Visual Experience.* New York: Harry N. Abrams, Inc., 1971.

Fish, Stanley. "Working on the Chain Gang: Interpretation in the Law and in Literary Criticism." *Critical Inquiry* 9 (1982): 201-216.

———. *Is There a Text in This Class?* Cambridge: Harvard University Press, 1980.

Fisher, Berenice. "Master Teacher Robert Ellis Dunn: Cultivating Creative Impulse." *Dance Magazine* 58, no. 1 (1984): 84-87.

Foster, Susan. *Reading Dancing: Bodies and Subjects in Contemporary American Dance.* Los Angeles: University of California Press, 1986.

Fraleigh, Sondra. "A Vulnerable Glance: Seeing Dance through Phenomenology." *Dance Research Journal* 23, no. 1 (1991): 11-16.

Friesen, Joanna. "Aesthetic Order in Dance." *Aesthetics and Dance.* AAHPERD Publications, 1980. 11-14.

———. "Perceiving Dance." *Journal of Aesthetic Education* 9 (1975): 97-108.

Frondizi, Risieri. *What is Value?* La Salle, IL: Open Court, 1971.

Gardner, Howard. "Multiple Intelligences: Implications for Artistic Creativity." In *Artistic Intelligences*, edited by William J. Moody, 11-27. New York: Teachers College Press, 1990.

———. *The Arts and Human Development.* New York: John Wiley and Sons, 1973.

Gates, Alice. "The Indirect Approach to Composition." *Impulse* 55 (1955): 5-9.

Gaut, Berys. "Interpreting the Arts: The Patchwork Theory." *Journal of Aesthetics and Art Criticism* 51, no. 4 (1993): 597-609.

Geahigan, George. "Linguistic Acts, Aesthetic Criticism, and Curriculum Policy." *Journal of Aesthetic Education* 16, no. 4 (1982): 13-26.

———. "Feldman on Evaluation." *Journal of Aesthetic Education* 9, no. 4 (1975): 29-42.

Getzels, Jacob W., and Mihaly Csikszentmihalyi. *The Creative Vision.* New York: John Wiley and Sons, 1976.

Gilbert, John V., ed. *Qualitative Evaluation in the Arts.* Proceedings of the Second and Third Institutes on Qualitative Evaluation in the Arts. New York: New York University Division of Arts and Arts Education, 1982.

Green, Thomas F. *The Activities of Teaching.* New York: McGraw-Hill, 1971.

Greene, Maxine. "Aesthetic Education and the Dance." In *Philosophical Essays on Dance,* edited by Gordon Fancher and Gerald Myers, 16-32. New York: Dance Horizons, 1981.

Greene, Theodore. *The Arts and the Art of Criticism.* Princeton: Princeton University Press, 1940.

Grossmann, Reinhardt. *Phenomenology and Existentialism.* London: Routledge and Kegan Paul, 1984.

Halprin, Anna. "Intuition and Improvisation in Dance." *Impulse* 55 (1955): 10-12.

Hamblen, Karen A. "'Don't You Think Some Brighter Colors Would Improve Your Painting?' - Or, Constructing Questions for Art Dialogues." *Art Education* 36, no. 2 (1983): 12-14.

Handbook for Instructors 1991. Expository Writing Program. New York University. David Hoover, Director.

Hanna, Judith Lynne. "The Mentality and Matter of Dance." *Art Education* 36, no. 2 (1983): 42-46.

Hanstein, Penelope. "On the Nature of Art Making in Dance: An Artistic Process Skills Model." PhD diss., Ohio State University, 1986.

Hawkins, Alma. *Creating Through Dance.* Rev. ed. Pennington, NJ: Princeton Book, 1988.

Hawkins, Erick. "Erick Hawkins Addresses a New-to-Dance Audience." In *The Dance Experience,* edited by Myron Howard Nadel and Constance Nadel Miller, 208-212. New York: Universe Books, 1978.

Hayes, Elizabeth R. *Dance Composition and Production.* New York: A.S. Barnes, 1955.

Hazlitt, Henry. *The Anatomy of Criticism*. New York: Simon and Schuster, 1933.

H'Doubler, Margaret. *Dance: A Creative Art Experience*. New York: F.S. Crofts, 1940.

Heyl, Bernard C. "The Critic's Reasons." *Journal of Aesthetics and Art Criticism* 16 (1957): 169-179.

———. *New Bearings in Esthetics and Art Criticism*. New Haven: Yale University Press, 1943.

Hirsch. E.D. *The Aims of Interpretation*. Chicago: University of Chicago Press, 1978.

———. *Validity in Interpretation*. New Haven, CN: Yale University Press, 1967.

Hobsbaum, Philip. *Theory of Criticism*. Bloomington: Indiana University Press, 1970.

Hodgens, Pauline. "Evaluating the Dance." In Adshead, Janet, et al. *Dance Analysis: Theory and Practice*. London: Dance Books, Ltd. 1988, 90-106.

Horst, Louis, and Carroll Russell. *Modern Dance Forms*. San Francisco: Impulse, 1961.

Horton-Fraleigh, Sondra. *Dance and the Lived Body - A Descriptive Aesthetics*. Pittsburgh: University of Pittsburgh Press, 1987.

——— "Aesthetic Perception in Dance." *Aesthetics and Dance*. AAHPERD Publications, 1980. 24-26.

Humphrey, Doris. *The Art of Making Dances*. New York: Grove Press, Inc., 1959.

Hungerland, Helmut. "Suggestions for Procedure in Art Criticism." *Journal of Aesthetics and Art Criticism* 4, no. 3 (1947): 189-195.

Hungerland, Isabel C. "The Concept of Intention in Art Criticism." *Journal of Philosophy* 52 (1955): 733-742.

Husserl, Edmund. *Ideas: General Introduction to Pure Phenomenology*. Translated by W.R. Boyce Gibson. New York: Collier Books, 1913/1962.

Ihde, Don. *Experimental Phenomenology*. New York: State University of New York Press, 1986.

Ingarden, Roman. "Artistic and Aesthetic Values." *British Journal of Aesthetics* 4, no. 3 (1964): 198-213.

Isenberg, Arnold. "Critical Communication." In *Art and Philosophy*, 2nd ed., edited by W.E. Kennick, 658-668. New York: St. Martin's Press, 1979.

———. *Aesthetics and the Theory of Criticism*. Chicago: University of Chicago Press, 1973.

———. "Perception, Meaning, and the Subject-Matter of Art." *The Journal of Philosophy* 41 (1944): 561-575.

Jessup, Bertram. "Taste and Judgment in Aesthetic Experience." In *The Dance Experience*, edited by Myron Howard Nadel and Constance Nadel Miller, 197-207. New York: Universe Books, 1978.

Johnstone, Jill. "Abstraction in Dance." *Dance Observer* 24 (1957): 151- 152.

———. "The Modern Dance—Directions and Criticisms." *Dance Observer* 24 (1957): 55-56.

Jones, R.L., Jr. "Phenomenological Balance and Aesthetic Response." *Journal of Aesthetic Education* 13, no. 1 (1979): 93-106.

Kaelin, Eugene F. *An Aesthetics for Art Educators.* New York: Teachers College Press, 1989.

———. *Art and Existence.* Lewisburg: Bucknell University Press, 1970.

———. *An Existentialist Aesthetic.* Madison: University of Wisconsin Press, 1966.

Kleinman, Seymour. "Phenomenology and the Dance." *Journal of Aesthetic Education* 2, no. 4 (1968): 125-130.

Knapp, Steven, and Walter Benn Michaels. *Against Theory.* Chicago: University of Chicago Press, 1982.

Kneller, George F. *Existentialism and Education.* New York: Philosophical Library, 1958.

Kerner, Mary. *Barefoot to Balanchine—How to Watch Dance.* New York: Anchor Books, 1990.

Kisselgoff, Anna. "Divining the Mystique of Mark Morris." *New York Times* 11 November 1990.

Kurfiss, Joanne G. *Critical Thinking: Theory, Research, Practice, and Possibilities.* ASHE-ERIC Higher Education Report No. 2. Washington, DC: Association for the Study of Higher Education, 1988.

Kuspit, Donald B. "Art Criticism: Where's the Depth?" *Artforum* 16, no. 1 (1977): 38-41.

Laban, Rudolf. *The Mastery of Movement.* Boston: Plays, Inc., 1971.

Langer, Susanne K. *Problems of Art.* New York: Charles Scribner's Sons, 1957.

———. *Feeling and Form.* New York: Charles Scribner's Sons, 1953.

Lavender, Larry. "Understanding Interpretation." *Dance Research Journal* 27, no. 2 (1995): 25-33.

———. "Critical Evaluation in the Choreography Class." *Dance Research Journal* 24, no. 2 (1992): 33-39.

Lavender, Larry, and Wendy Oliver. "Learning to 'See' Dance: The Role of Critical Writing in Developing Students' Aesthetic Awareness." *Impulse* 1, no. 1 (1993): 10-20.

Levin, David Michael. "Philosophers and the Dance." In *What is Dance?*, edited by Roger Copeland and Marshall Cohen, 85-94. Oxford: Oxford University Press, 1983.

Lillback, Elna. "An Approach to Dance Composition." *Journal of Health and Physical Education* 12, no. 2 (1941): 83-85.

Lippincott, Gertrude. "The Function of the Teacher in Modern Dance Composition." *Journal of Health and Physical Education* 16, no. 9 (1954): 497.

Lockhart, Aileene S., and Esther E. Pease. *Modern Dance—Building and Teaching Lessons.* 6th ed. Dubuque, IA: William C. Brown, 1982.

Lord, Madeline. "A Characterization of Dance Teacher Behaviors in Technique and Choreography Classes." *Dance Research Journal* 14, no. 1 (1981-82): 15-31.

Mackinnon, Donald W. "What Makes a Person Creative?" In *The Dance Experience,* edited by Myron Howard Nadel and Constance Nadel Miller, 59-67. New York: Universe Books, 1978.

Mains, Margaret. "Qualities of Dance Movement." *Journal of Health and Physical Education* 18, no. 2 (1947): 72-74.

Maletic, Vera. *Body-Space-Expression.* Berlin: Mouton de Gruyter, 1987.

Margolis, Joseph. "Reinterpreting Interpretation." *Journal of Aesthetics and Art Criticism* 47, no. 3 (1989): 237-251.

———. "Recent Work on Aesthetics." In *Recent Work in Philosophy,* edited by Kenneth G. Lucey. Totowa, NJ: Rowman and Allanheld, 1983.

———. "Aesthetic Perception." *Journal of Aesthetics and Art Criticism* 19, no. 2 (1960): 209-213.

Martin, John. *Introduction to the Dance.* New York: Dance Horizons, 1968.

———. *The Modern Dance.* New York: Dance Horizons, 1933.

Matthews, Robert J. "Describing and Interpreting a Work of Art." *Journal of Aesthetics and Art Criticism* 36, no. 1 (1977): 5-14.

May, Rollo. *The Courage to Create.* New York: Bantam, 1980.

Meeson, Phillip. "The Imagination in Art and Art Education." *Journal of Aesthetic Education* 9, no. 4 (1975): 55-68.

Merleau-Ponty, Maurice. *Phenomenology of Perception.* Translated by Colin Smith. London: Routledge and Kegan Paul, 1962.

Metheney, Eleanor, and Lois Ellfeldt. "Symbolic Forms of Movement: Dance." In *The Dance Experience,* edited by Myron Howard Nadel and Constance Nadel Miller, 49-54. New York: Universe Books, 1978.

Mettler, Barbara. *Group Dance Improvisations.* Tucson: Mettler Studios, 1975.

———. *Materials of Dance as a Creative Art Activity.* Tucson: Mettler Studios, 1960.

Meux, Milton. "Teaching the Act of Evaluating." *Journal of Aesthetic Education* 8, no. 1 (1974): 85-105.

Minton, Sandra Cerney. *Choreography*. Champaign, IL: Human Kinetics, 1986.

———. *Modern Dance: Body and Mind*. Englewood, CO: Norton Publishing Co., 1984.

Montague, Phillip. "Learning Aesthetic Concepts and Justifying Aesthetic Judgments." *Journal of Aesthetic Education* 13, no. 1 (1979): 45-52.

Morgenroth, Joyce. *Dance Improvisations*. Pittsburgh: University of Pittsburgh Press, 1987.

Moustakas, Clark. *Creativity and Conformity*. New York: D. Van Norstrand, 1967.

Myers, Gerald. "Do You See What the Critic Sees?" In *Philosophical Essays on Dance*, edited by Gordon Fancher and Gerald Myers, 33-68. New York: Dance Horizons, 1981.

Nadel, Myron Howard. "The Audience and the Choreographer: A Sense of Responsibility." In *The Dance Experience*, edited by Myron Howard Nadel and Constance Nadel Miller, 213-215. New York: Universe Books, 1978.

———. "The Process of Creating a Dance." In *The Dance Experience*, edited by Myron Howard Nadel and Constance Nadel Miller, 74-81. New York: Universe Books, 1978.

Nahm, Milton C. *Readings in Philosophy of Art and Aesthetics*. Englewood Cliffs, NJ: Prentice-Hall, 1975.

Neel, Jasper. *Plato, Derrida, and Writing*. Carbondale, IL: Southern Illinois University Press, 1988.

Newick, Shula. "The Experience of Aloneness in Making Art." *Journal of Aesthetic Education* 16, no. 2 (1982): 65-74.

Osborne, Harold. *Aesthetics and Criticism*. Westport, CN: Greenwood Press, 1973.

———. "Taste and Judgment in the Arts." *Journal of Aesthetic Education* 5, no. 4 (1971): 13-28.

Parsons, M. J. "The Skill of Appreciation." *Journal of Aesthetic Education* 7, no. 1 (1973): 75-82.

Patrick, Catharine. "Creative Thought in Artists." *Journal of Psychology* 4 (1937): 35-73.

Pease, Esther E. *Modern Dance*. Dubuque, IA: William C. Brown, 1966.

Penrod, James, and Janice Gudde Plastino. *The Dancer Prepares*. Palo Alto, CA: National Press Books, 1970.

Pepper, Stephen. "The Concept of Fusion in Dewey's Aesthetic Theory." *Journal of Aesthetics and Art Criticism* 12, no. 2 (1953): 169-176.

———. *The Basis of Criticism in the Arts*. Cambridge, MA.: Harvard University Press, 1949.

Perkins, David. "Talk About Art." In *Arts and Aesthetics: An Agenda for the Future*, edited by Stanley S. Madeja, 279-304. St. Louis: CEMREL, 1977.

———. "Theory in Arts Education." *Journal of Aesthetic Education* 11, no. 1 (1977): 5-18.

Perkins, David. *The Mind's Best Work*. Cambridge: Harvard University Press. 1981.

Prall, D.W. *Aesthetic Analysis*. New York: Thomas Y. Crowell Co., 1936.

———. *Aesthetic Judgment*. New York: Thomas Y. Crowell Co., 1929.

Preston-Dunlop, Valery. *A Handbook for Modern Educational Dance*. Boston: Plays, Inc., 1980.

Puravs, Olgerts. "Criticism and Experience." *Journal of Aesthetic Education* 7, no. 1 (1973): 11-22.

Radir, Ruth Anderson. *Modern Dance for the Youth of America*. New York: A.S. Barnes and Co., 1945.

Redfern, Hildred Betty. *Questions in Aesthetic Education*. London: Unwin Hyman, Ltd., 1986.

———. *Concepts in Modern Educational Dance*. London: Dance Books Ltd., 1982.

Rowe, Patricia A. "Identification of the Domain of Modern Dance Choreography as an Aesthetic Discipline." PhD diss., Stanford University, 1966.

Ryle, Gilbert. *The Concept of Mind*. London: Hutchinson and Company, Ltd., 1949.

Schlaich, Joan, and Betty Dupont. *Dance: The Art of Production*. 2nd ed. Pennington, NJ: Princeton Book Company Publishers, 1988.

Shafranski, Paulette. *Modern Dance: Twelve Creative Problem-Solving Experiments*. Glenview, IL: Scott, Foresman and Company, 1985.

Shahn, Ben. *The Shape of Content*. Cambridge, MA: Harvard University Press, 1957.

Sheets, Maxine. *The Phenomenology of Dance*. Madison: University of Wisconsin Press, 1966.

Sheets-Johnstone, Maxine., ed. *Illuminating Dance*. Lewisburg: Bucknell University Press, 1984.

———. "Thinking in Movement." *Journal of Aesthetics and Art Criticism* 39 (1980): 399-407.

Sherbon, Elizabeth. *On the Count of One: Modern Dance Methods*. 2nd ed. Palo Alto, CA: Mayfield, 1975.

Shusterman, Richard. *Pragmatist Aesthetics*. Cambridge: Blackwell, 1992.

———. "Interpretation, Intention, and Truth." *Journal of Aesthetics and Art Criticism* 46 (1988): 399-411.

————. "The Logic of Interpretation." *Philosophical Quarterly* 28 (1978): 310-324.

Siegel, Marcia B. "The Truth About Apples and Oranges." *The Drama Review* 32, no. 3 (1988): 24-31.

————. "The Education of a Dance Critic: The Bonsai and the Lumberjack." *Dance Scope* 15, no. 1 (1981): 16-21.

Sirridge, Mary and Adina Armelagos. "The In's and Out's of Dance: Expression as an Aspect of Style." *Journal of Aesthetics and Art Criticism* 36, no. 1 (1977): 15-24.

Smith, Jacqueline M. *Dance Composition—A Practical Guide for Teachers*. Surrey: Lepus Books, 1976.

Smith, Nancy W., ed. *Focus on Dance IV*. Reston, VA: American Association for Health, Physical Education and Recreation, 1969.

Smith, Ralph. "Teaching Aesthetic Criticism in the Schools." *Journal of Aesthetic Education* 7, no. 1 (1973): 38-49.

————. *Aesthetics and Criticism in Art Education*. Chicago: Rand McNally, 1966.

————, ed. *Aesthetic Concepts and Education*. Urbana: University of Illinois Press, 1970.

————, and Alan Simpson, eds. *Aesthetics and Arts Education*. Urbana: University of Illinois Press, 1991.

————, and C. M. Smith. "The Artworld and Aesthetic Skills: A Context for Research and Development." In *Arts and Aesthetics*, edited by Stanley S. Madeja, 305-316. St. Louis: CEMREL, Inc., 1977.

Snoeyenbos, Milton H., and Carole A. Knapp. "Dance Theory and Dance Education." *Journal of Aesthetic Education* 13, no. 3 (1979): 17-30.

Sontag, Susan. *Against Interpretation*. New York: Anchor Books, 1990.

Sorrell, Walter. "To Be a Critic." In *The Dance Experience*, edited by Myron Howard Nadel and Constance Nadel Miller, 216-225. New York: Universe Books, 1978.

Souriau, Etienne. "A General Methodology for the Scientific Study of Aesthetic Appreciation." *Journal of Aesthetics and Art Criticism* 14, no. 1 (1955): 1-18.

Sparshott, Francis. "On the Question: 'Why do Philosophers Neglect the Aesthetics of the Dance?'" *Dance Research Journal* 15, no. 1 (1982): 5-23.

Spiegelberg, Herbert. *Doing Phenomenology*. The Hague: Martinus Jijhoff, 1975.

Stecker, Robert. "Relativism about Interpretation." *Journal of Aesthetics and Art Criticism* 53, no. 1 (1995): 14-18.

Tompkins, Jane P., ed. *Reader Response Criticism*. Baltimore: Johns Hopkins University Press, 1980.

Tormey, Alan. "Critical Judgments." In *Art and Philosophy* 2nd ed., edited by W.E. Kennick, 620-630. New York: St. Martin's Press, 1979.

Turner, Margery J. *Approaches to Nonliteral Choreography.* Pittsburgh: University of Pittsburgh Press, 1971.

van Mancn, Max. *The Tact of Teaching.* New York: State University of New York Press, 1991.

Vivas, Eliseo, and Murray Krieger, eds. *The Problems of Aesthetics.* New York: Holt, Rinehart and Winston, 1966.

Walker, Diane, and Cynthia Rostankowski. "Effort/Shape Theory and the Aesthetics of Dance." *Aesthetics and Dance.* AAHPERD Publications, 1980. 15-17.

Weisberg, Robert W. *Creativity, Genius, and Other Myths.* New York: W.H. Freeman and Co., 1986.

Weitz, Morris. "The Role of Theory in Aesthetics." *Journal of Aesthetics and Art Criticism,* 14, no. 1 (1956): 27-35.

————. "Criticism Without Evaluation." In *Problems in Criticism of the Arts,* edited by Holley Gene Duffield, 277-284. San Francisco: Chandler Publishing Co., 1968.

————. *Philosophy of the Arts.* New York: Russell and Russell, 1964.

————. "Reasons in Criticism." *Journal of Aesthetics and Art Criticism* 20, no. 4 (1962): 429-437.

Wimsatt, W.K., Jr., and Monroe C. Beardsley. "The Affective Fallacy." *Sewanee Review* 57 (1949): 31-55.

————. "The Intentional Fallacy." In *Philosophy Looks at the Arts,* edited by Joseph Margolis, 367-380. Philadelphia: Temple University Press, 1987.

Ziff, Paul. "About the Appreciation of Dance." In *Philosophical Essays on Dance,* edited by Gordon Rancher and Gerald Myers, 69-94. New York: Dance Horizons, 1981.

INDEX

A

Adshead, Janet 74
Ambiguity in art, 84
Analysis, 73-75, 81
Anticritical beliefs, 122-125
Argumentative criticism, 83
Armelagos, Adina, 40
Artistic Assumptions, 72-73
Artworld, 20, 33
Assessment of student critics, 133-134

B

Best, David, 42-44
Blom, Lynne Anne, 112, 117
Boas, George, 56

C

Casual conversation
  and critical discourse, 13-15
Chaplin, L. Tarin, 112, 117
Choreography, process of, 16-17
  advanced level, 116-118
  beginning level, 112-116
Communication, theory of, 40-41
  linguistic, 42-43
  perceptual, 43-44
Critical disagreement, 125-130
  causes of, 127
  remedy for, 130
Critical discussion, 13-15, 80-87
  artists' contribution to, 84-87
Critical evaluation, 1
  and artists' intentions, 40-47
  and predetermined criteria, 32-27
  and subjectivism, 24-29
  as a goal, ix
  as a language art, 3-4
  as a method, ix
  obstacles to, 122-130
  perspectives on, 9-20

Critical projection, 102, 115-116
Critical thinking, 4-5
Critical writing, 5-6, 68-69
Criticism, argumentative,
  exploratory, 68
  in aesthetic inquiry, 95-96
Csikszentmihalyi, Mihaly, 113, 118

D

Definitions, problems with, 128
Description, 70-81
  in evaluation, 93
  language of, 71-72
Discovered problems, 114, 118-119
Discussion. See Critical discussion

E

Ecker, David W., 94
Eisner, Elliot W., 90
Emotions
  in art, 27
  of viewers, 24-29
Evaluation, 90-99
Exaggerations, 129
Explanations, 85-86
Exploratory criticism, 68
External information about art, 46
Extrinsic features of art, 74

F

Feldman, Edmund B., 68, 70, 73, 82
Focused freewriting, 69

G

Gardner, Howard, 24-25
Getzels, Jacob W., 113, 118
Green, Thomas F., 90-91

H

Heyl, Bernard C., 128-129
High-inference language, 71
Hodgens, Pauline, 28
Humphrey, Doris, 54

I

Idealist notion, 18-19
Indoctrination, and instruction, 52
Intentions, of artists, 40-47
    use of in critical evaluation, 44-46
    versus meaning, 46
Internal information about art, 46
Interpretation, 3, 82-87

J

Judgments, 26-27, 90-94
    and facts, 91
    and feelings, 91
    comparative, 93-94
    competing, 92
Justifications, artistic, 85-86

K

Kaelin, Eugene F., 94
Knapp, Carole, 73
Kurfiss, Joanne G., 5

L

Laban, Rudolf, 75
Ladder of Aesthetic Inquiry, 94
    and criticism, 95-96
    and metacriticism, 96-97
    and metatheory, 97-98
    and theory, 97-98
Linguistic Communication, 42-43
Low-inference language, 71

M

Metacriticism. *See* Ladder of Aesthetic
    Inquiry
Metatheory. *See* Ladder of Aesthetic
    Inquiry

N

Noticing, and recognizing, 63

O

Observation, 2, 61-65
Openness, perceptual, 62

P

Pease, Esther, 35
Perceptual communication, 43-44
Perkins, David, 63, 93, 105-106, 127-128
Picasso, Pablo, 16
Post-revisions review, 104-105
Predetermined criteria, dangers of, 32-36
Presented problems, 113-114

R

Referential adequacy, of critical claims, 83
Reflection, 68-77
Reflective writing, 67-68
Revisions, process of art, 16-18
    recommendation of, 102-106

S

Self-censorship, 124
Self-evaluation, 56
Siegel, Marcia, 114
Sirridge, Mary, 40
Smith, Jaqueline M., 26
Smith, Ralph, 68, 83
Snoeyenbos, Milton, 73
Subjective response, 24-29

T

Teaching Hints
    clarifying questions, 85
    critical discussions, 80
    levels of discourse, 97
    making judgments, 92
    overcoming defensiveness, 106
    reflective writing, 70
    shifting the focus of discussion, 103
Teaching principles, list of, 60
    artists' intentions, 47
    fostering reflection and debate, 52
    predetermined criteria, 37
    students' role as critics, 53
    subjective response, 30
"Think on it" prompts
    artistic intentions, 19
    creative and critical mind, 18
    critical talk, 15
    explaining the meaning of art, 44
    hearing feedback, 107
    heightened consciousness, 64
    letter to a critic, 99
    liking and disliking art, 27
    loaded and unloaded language, 72
    making and evaluating dances, 13
    reflective thinking, 76
    standards of judgment, 34
    the creative experience, 42

V

Vagueness in art, 129

W

Weitz, Morris, 126

ABOUT THE AUTHOR

Larry Lavender is Head of Dance at the University of New Mexico. He has taught dance at New York University, the University of Missouri at Kansas City, and the University of California at Irvine. He also has choreographed more than 30 dances and composed music for many of them. In 1984 he received the Distinguished Student Scholar Award from UC-Irvine for his original choreography and music of "The Sleep of Reason."

Lavender has taught criticism to dance students across the United States and around the world, including England, Mexico, and New Zealand. He has published numerous articles on dance criticism for journals such as *Impulse, Dance Research Journal,* and *Focus on Dance.* Lavender earned a BA in humanities and a BA in dance from

UC-Riverside, and an MFA in fine arts and dance from UC-Irvine. In 1993 he completed his PhD in dance and dance education at New York University.

He is on the board of directors of the Congress on Research in Dance and is a member of the National Dance Association and the National Arts Education Association.

Lavender lives in Albuquerque, New Mexico, with his wife, Elisabeth, and their daughter, Bridget. He enjoys hiking, music, and reading.

Other Dance Resources

Foreword by Judith B. Alter
1994 • Paper • 216 pp
Item BSCH0530 • ISBN 0-87322-530-9
$22.00 ($32.95 Canadian)

Learn the many benefits of movement improvisation, the principles involved in teaching it, and the techniques used to stimulate it. Discover how to conduct a creative movement class, including tips on building trust and establishing group unity.

The book features 163 classroom-tested themes, which are excellent for eliciting impromptu responses and 136 illuminating quotations from student interviews over the years. These themes are categorized by experience level, number of participants, and purpose. All of the themes are presented in an easy-to-use table that helps you quickly find an appropriate theme.

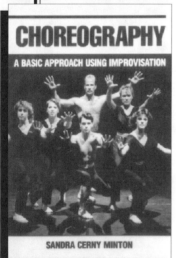

1986 • Paper • 144 pp
Item BMIN0071 • ISBN 0-87322-071-4
$20.00 ($29.95 Canadian)

Take the mystery out of choreography with this excellent how-to book. Learn the basics of dance composition for designing and shaping a dance, improvising, and performing. The valuable suggestions on selecting accompaniment, designing costumes, and planning lighting will help produce informal or professional performances. No matter what your interest in choreography, you can apply this book to your special needs.

To request more information or to place your order, U.S. customers call
TOLL-FREE 1-800-747-4457. Customers outside the U.S. use appropriate telephone
number/address shown in the front of this book.

Human Kinetics
The Information Leader in Physical Activity
2335